A JOHN CATT PUBLICATION

C000064485

THE SCHOOL
LEADERSHIP
JOURNEY

JOHN DUNFORD

Toby,

It's been great to share
my leadership journey
with you. Thanks for
all you do for the
education service.

Best wishes,

John

16·xi·16

"A book of remarkable breadth and depth"
Geoff Barton

First Published 2016

by John Catt Educational Ltd,
12 Deben Mill Business Centre, Old Maltings Approach,
Melton, Woodbridge IP12 1BL

Tel: +44 (0) 1394 389850 Fax: +44 (0) 1394 386893
Email: enquiries@johncatt.com
Website: www.johncatt.com

ISBN: 978 1 909717 91 6

Set and designed by John Catt Educational Limited

John Dunford Consulting

jd@johndunfordconsulting.co.uk
Mobile: 07710 039139 Tel: 01858 881108
Cobblestones, Church Street, North Kilworth, Leicestershire LE17 6EZ
www.johndunfordconsulting.co.uk

Toby,

I hope you can recommend the book to school leaders in the OAT.

With compliments

John

"There are many books about school and system leadership. John Dunford's text is distinctive because of its magisterial scope. It ranges across the big policy issues of government and then tracks how these impact on schools. The result is a book of remarkable breadth and depth, a call-to-arms to hold on to our moral purpose as school leaders. It's as uplifting as it is persuasive. I can't recommend it highly enough." – Geoff Barton, head of King Edward VI School, Bury St Edmunds

"Politically astute, highly experienced and strongly principled, John Dunford is one of the most knowledgeable and wise figures in education today. With his typical warmth, clarity, humility and strong moral purpose, he brings together insights from his personal experience and wide reading to create a commentary on education broad in scope and deep in understanding." – Dr Jill Berry, leadership consultant and former head

"A natural story-teller, John Dunford illustrates, through vivid accounts of his leadership story, insights into what it takes to be an enabling leader true to principle and values and restlessly determined to move things on." – Sir Tim Brighouse, former London Schools Commissioner

"I just love this book. John Dunford weaves an informed narrative about what really matters in schools and will give any school leader both great insight and the confidence to do the very best for their pupils. Reflecting John's huge experience in schools and his interactions with governments, he gives a unique perspective on our educational system. A must-read for any school leader." – Andy Buck, founder and managing director of Leadership Matters

"No matter where you are on your leadership journey this book provides invaluable insight into the key ingredients of school leadership. John's experience and expertise are evident throughout." – Sian Carr, president of the Association of School and College Leaders, 2016/17 and executive principal of Skinners' Kent Academy

"John has unrivalled knowledge, understanding and expertise in navigating our system's opportunities and challenges. He remains optimistic about what school leaders at all levels can achieve if they stay true to their values. He writes with real passion, providing a route-map for the future." – David Crossley, associate director of Whole Education

"This book is a gift of wisdom to any school leader seeking deeper understanding of the often confusing English system of education. Those new to school leadership will particularly appreciate the perceptive insights synthesised from his vast experience and current voices of evidence-informed sense." – Stef Edwards, head of Great Bowden Academy and CEO of Learn Academies Trust

"John Dunford brings to this book his boundless passion for education, his commitment to enhancing the life chances of young people and his wealth of experience as a school leader. He fluently analyses the key developments in education policy during his professional lifetime and uses the learning from his own leadership journey to offer practical advice for school leaders." – Robert Hill, Visiting Professor, UCL Institute of Education and former policy adviser in No 10 Downing Street and the Department for Education

"There are few people better qualified than John Dunford to reflect on the challenges of school leadership. This book is both thoughtful and thought provoking. It will help school leaders and all those passionate about education to look beyond the pressures of Ofsted and accountability, to reflect on what education should be about and how to improve its quality." – Rt Hon David Laws, executive chair of the Education Policy Institute and former minister for schools

"John Dunford ranks amongst the wisest and most highly respected voices in education whose experience spans many years in schools and at the highest levels of the education system. As well as providing deep insight into education policy, this book reaches the heart of improving the life chances of young people." – Brian Lightman, former general secretary, Association of School and College Leaders

"Few people in education have had such a fascinating leadership journey as John Dunford. In this book he talks with authority, wisdom and, most of all, authenticity about leadership in schools and across the system." – Steve Munby, chief executive of the Education Development Trust and former chief executive of the National College for School Leadership

"John Dunford shares his extensive knowledge of the world of English education, gained from his unique experience as a system-leader over many years. This book provides leadership stories and insight whilst maintaining an over-arching commentary on the education landscape. Hugely enjoyable!" – Dame Alison Peacock, CEO of the Chartered College of Teaching

"Navigating the stormy waters of education policy feels like crossing the Atlantic using dead reckoning under a cloudy sky. This brilliant book provides a perfect companion for the journey. Whatever the reader's stage of leadership, this book should be at the top of the list." – Marc Rowland, deputy director of the National Education Trust

"A great resource for any serving or aspiring school leader. The book has optimism, deep knowledge, a strong narrative and some very practical guidance. John's passion, knowledge, positivity, practicality and experience come through in every chapter." – Brett Wigdortz, CEO of Teach First

Contents

For my wife, Sue, and
for Alastair, Ashley, Rachel and Rebecca
and the grandchildren

Introduction

This book is about school leadership, but it is not a leadership manual. I have never been a theoretician about leadership, but have learned from others along the way. The aim is to share some of the learning gained on my leadership journey in order to help school leaders chart a course for their schools and for their own professional development through the choppy waters of national education policy.

The starting point was a blog post I wrote in 2011 entitled 'Ten things I have learned on my leadership journey'. These are not particularly profound, nor are they backed by references to the great works on educational leadership, but they are things that have helped me and which have struck a chord with some people who have read them.

My leadership journey in education started at school and took an interesting turn when I was president of the union at Nottingham University in 1968-69, a year in which student revolution was spreading rapidly from California to UK universities and from which even the largely conservative Nottingham was not immune. As a moderate president, caught between some activist far-left students and university authorities slow to embrace change, I learned a lot about leadership in a short time, with my youthful mistakes providing some pretty sharp and uncomfortable lessons. It felt as if, at the age of 21, I had had five years' experience in a single year.

After a rather poor postgraduate certificate in education course, I started teaching in 1970, and discovered that I had had a lot more experience of leadership and of the committee work that goes with it than my fellow young teachers. With the national shortage of mathematics teachers in the early 1970s, I found myself as head of mathematics in a sizeable comprehensive school, Framwellgate Moor in Durham City, at the age of 26 after only three years of teaching.

Three months later, in January 1974, the Framwellgate Moor head, who had himself been a students' union president 30 years earlier, appointed me to the additional post of senior teacher (assistant head, in modern parlance). This brought with it a place on the leadership team of one of the most forward-looking comprehensive schools in the north of England. My responsibilities included the curriculum, the school timetable and cover for absent staff. But it was the collective responsibility of being part of the school leadership team, as well as leading the mathematics department, that gave me some of the most formative, exhilarating and exhausting years of my career.

It was a wrench to leave a school where I had given and learned so much and made so many good friendships, but my breadth of responsibility at Framwellgate Moor had given me a taste for school leadership and a strong desire to put my ideas into action as a deputy head and head. I did not enjoy my three years of being a deputy as much as being a head of department, but there was much to be done at Bede School, Sunderland, which was struggling to move from its long history as a grammar school – 'The Bede', as it was known locally – to a neighbourhood comprehensive school serving some tough parts of the town. Apart from learning a lot about behaviour management, which took up a high proportion of every working day, my responsibilities included curriculum development. The school needed to move beyond the grammar school curriculum it had continued to teach to its very different student population. This required a change of culture. It was a challenging task with the senior and middle leaders having had long experience of teaching in grammar schools and nowhere else, unleavened by the professional development that should have been a top priority when the school changed status. There was some good teaching, but nowhere near as much as at Framwellgate Moor, and some truly awful teaching. I recall one lesson in particular in which the head of biology stood at a lectern and read out his university notes to a class of lower sixth formers.

My reason for observing that lesson was to monitor the language levels being used across the curriculum. The Bullock report, *A language for life*, had been published in 1975 and it was very clear that nobody at Bede School had implemented it, or had even read it. Teachers in all subjects used language in their teaching or in textbooks that learners with a reading age at or below their chronological age could not understand. It was hardly surprising so much time was spent on behaviour management.

My frustration in the role of deputy head was that the more innovations I made the more I found myself running them, as the management structure of the school did not allow the space for people to work with me and to share the joy and challenge of change management. It was a lesson I took with me into headship.

Around the age of 30, I had applied for 14 deputy headships and been interviewed for eight before I got the job at Bede. The step up to headship proved easier, with success coming at my fourth interview, a considerably less thorough process in 1982 than is now the case. I was given 17 minutes to answer a single question and three minutes to add any further information. Any candidate unwise enough to get his or her timing wrong was interrupted mid-sentence. The appointment committee, comprising Durham County councillors and members of the school governing body – but only those who were active in the Labour Party – took less than three minutes to come to a decision, with the chief education officer not allowed to speak prior to the vote being taken.

I felt a huge sense of shock, responsibility and fear. I had visited the school, although it would have been possible to have been appointed without having done so, and indeed, not all the interviewed candidates had taken up the offer of a visit. It was a truly terrible system for appointing headteachers, although an improvement on drawing the names of equally qualified interviewees out of a tea cosy, which had occurred at a County Durham school a few years earlier. It was eight years later, with the advent of local management of schools, that schools began to design their own, more rigorous, appointment processes.

This began 16 years of headship at Durham Johnston Comprehensive School, which grew from 1200 to 1500 pupils in that time and gave its students a quality of education rich in both breadth and depth. The experience of those 16 years weaves its way into all the following chapters, so it need not be repeated here. Suffice it to say that I regard myself as extremely fortunate to have had the opportunity to lead such a great school, with so many excellent staff, a good number of whom are still at the school 18 years after I left. Durham Johnston was, and remains, (in the words of a *Daily Telegraph Good Schools' Guide* in the early 1990s) 'a quintessentially good comprehensive school' and the school has long been near the top of the non-selective school A level results tables. Looking back, there were things I could not, or did not, shift that should have been addressed more strongly, so, in the words of Frank Sinatra's song, 'Regrets, I've had a few...'

New Zealand rugby players speak eloquently of their attitude to playing for their country. Far from the arrogant selfishness of some other sporting stars, they are conscious throughout their international careers that they are merely custodians of the All Black shirt that bears the number of their position in the team, passing it on from the great players who preceded them to the future internationals who will wear it. I felt much the same about my time as head of Durham Johnston. The school had had just five heads in the 80 years up to 1982 and then I had the privilege of being the custodian of the head's office for 16 years before handing it on to others who would take the school to greater heights.

Opportunities to work outside the school were not open to headteachers in the 1980s in the way they are in the school-led system of the 21st century in England. So when one of the Durham secondary heads called me in 1988 and suggested I should stand for the national council of the Secondary Heads Association (SHA), I put my name forward and was elected as a representative of the north-east. Thus began a 22-year membership of a body that provided the best in-service training a school leader could have had, bringing back to school up-to-date news and examples of excellent practice from some of the best school leaders in the country. After a spell as chair of the association's education committee, working in particular on plans to improve 14-19 qualifications, I became SHA president, with a sabbatical year from school in 1995-96.

Two years later, in 1998, I was elected as SHA general secretary and moved from the north-east to Leicester, where the association had its headquarters. I have enjoyed every stage of my career, but the 12 years I spent at SHA (which became the Association of School and College Leaders (ASCL) in 2006) were the happiest and most fulfilling. Through evolution rather than revolution, the culture of the organisation changed from the old boys' club (and the key association people in 1998 were almost all men in their 50s) to a highly professional operation with a more mixed and younger membership, that was frequently quoted in the media and was influential on politicians of all parties. As with Durham Johnston, the leadership lessons I learned during my time with the association are threaded through the text of this book.

I saw the main part of my job as representing ASCL members' views to the government and its agencies, leaving most of the running of the association and the support of individual school leaders to the headquarters team and its field force. ASCL was in the business of changing public policy, so school leaders could implement sensible change at a manageable pace for the benefit of their pupils. Changing public policy is both an art and a science, and my ASCL colleagues and I were avid learners from those with experience in the field.

Being a union general secretary sometimes requires a delicate path to be trodden between the union members and the government, with the government pursuing its political and educational priorities, and pressure from the members whom one represents generally believing that the government is mistaken in its actions and that school leaders should be left well alone to run their schools.

A general secretary has to articulate those concerns, while gaining sufficient respect from those in power that they continue to want to talk, even when one is opposing their policies root and branch. The way in which to balance these demands was for the association to have a well-considered set of policies in all the major areas of government education activity. Then, when a policy was announced with which school leaders disagreed, I would not shout from the rooftop – as many union leaders have had a reputation for doing – 'It's all a load of rubbish', but instead would say, 'If you, the government, want to do this, then it would be much better if you did it this way, since that is the way in which school leaders can implement change most effectively', and then reiterate ASCL policy on the topic in a thinly disguised attempt to obtain changes in the government's line.

During the New Labour years, this proved reasonably effective most of the time, but that did not always please ASCL members, from some of whom I received vituperative emails asking why I had allowed the government to do such-and-such and demanding that I get it changed immediately. Like all unions, ASCL is a broad church; fortunately, supporters outweighed opponents and the ASCL leadership was able to conduct its business with government in a manner that obtained changes to bad policies, but ensured that ministers and officials continued to listen to us.

The year 2010 seemed a good time to retire as general secretary. I had been in the job for 12 years and, at the time I gave my notice, it seemed likely that there would be a different colour of government after the general election. The tightrope to be walked between the views of ASCL members and the government's plans would require a different approach with a Conservative government from that employed by ASCL during the New Labour years.

Retiring in my early 60s also gave me the opportunity to pursue a wide range of activities, which have formed an interesting additional part of my leadership journey. My first project came from an unexpected source. The secretary of state, Michael Gove, asked me in 2010 to conduct a review of the Office of the Children's Commissioner, the radical recommendations from which were accepted by the government and have subsequently passed into legislation.

My two years as national pupil premium champion, and continuing involvement in raising the attainment of disadvantaged young people and closing the gap with their more fortunate peers, have given me further insights into school leadership in one of its most challenging aspects.

I have learned that chairing an organisation is very different from being a chief executive and the chairmanship of the Chartered Institute of Educational Assessors and of Step Together Volunteering (formerly WorldWide Volunteering) have at times provided considerable challenges. Whole Education, which I have chaired since its inception in 2010, has been enormously stimulating, working with marvellous schools that are putting their curriculum ideals into practice.

That has been my leadership journey, but this book is not intended to be about me. While incorporating the lessons from this experience, the book is intended to be helpful to school leaders in developing policy and practice in their schools during a period when so much is changing so quickly in national education policy.

Every field of employment and public service undergoes change over time and it is naïve to expect that one can continue in any job without facing major changes. In a leadership position, dealing with the consequences of change and its implementation at institution level are a big part of the job description. However, the changes in schools' policy have some special factors that need to be taken into account in considering how to lead a successful school.

First, the volume, range and speed of change are as significant as the type of changes that governments have demanded of schools. This situation, replicated in almost every school year, has produced challenges for schools – especially smaller schools – in implementing change in several different fields simultaneously.

Second, the politicisation of education has introduced a high degree of instability into the policy-making process.

Third, pressures on schools are sometimes in conflict with both the government and the inspection agency, Ofsted, using accountability to drive policy and practice in schools, individually and collectively.

Fourth, education policy is contested territory, so there has rarely been sufficiently strong evidence to point the way forward, although there is now a much firmer and more accessible body of evidence to which school leaders and teachers (and government ministers) can look for guidance.

This book is designed to be read either from cover to cover or a chapter at a time, with each section focusing on a particular aspect of school leadership. The following overview of the content of each chapter is intended to help readers who wish to adopt the latter approach.

The first chapter stresses the importance of having a clear set of values to guide the leadership of the school, with examples from values-led schools and suggestions as to how school leaders can use values to take control of the education agenda in their school and not be overwhelmed by external factors.

This is dealt with in more detail in each of the subsequent chapters, with values underpinning decisions about the future structure of the school in chapter 2, the development of the curriculum in chapter 3 and the leadership of assessment in chapter 4.

Chapter 5 looks at accountability and suggests that leadership on this topic does not have to be reactive, but that accountability can be used proactively to reinforce the implementation of a vision and of values-based policies. Chapter 6 draws on my experience as national pupil premium champion to set out some thoughts on disadvantage and closing the gap, which are at the top of the education agenda in many countries, but especially in the UK, where the gap is wider than most. Chapter 7 is a discussion of professional and leadership development as the basis for the implementation of the ideas in other parts of the book.

Chapter 8 contains a discussion of school leadership at all levels, setting out 12 characteristics of successful leadership and stressing the opportunities existing for school leaders, even in a climate of central government prescription, to be creative and innovative. Chapter 9 welcomes the opportunities for system leadership in a school-led system and the concluding chapter draws together the themes of the book, putting school leadership in the wider context of public service reform and showing how confident and creative school leaders can take their schools to great heights of achievement that make a real difference to the life chances of the young people in their charge and influence the direction of national education policy.

Every chapter is, I hope, imbued with the last of the ten lessons learned on my leadership journey – the four Hs of school leadership: humanity, humility, hope and humour. School leaders at all levels need these in full measure if they are to lead happy and successful schools and to experience the joy and professional fulfilment of doing so.

Chapter 1

Values-led leadership

The aim of education is the knowledge,
not of facts, but of values.
William S. Burroughs

When your values are clear to you,
making decisions becomes easier.
Roy E. Disney

In 2012 I telephoned a headteacher I know well and spoke to him for the first time for a year or so. 'Hello, Steve, how are you?' I asked him. 'Not too bad. We had Ofsted 18 months ago and got a Good, and our exam results this summer were OK, so we should be clear of Ofsted for quite a while yet.' We continued our conversation about his challenging school and the interesting work in which he was involved as head of a co-operative trust school, but I reflected afterwards on that answer to my first question. Have we really reached a stage where a successful headteacher of a challenging school defines the state of his health with an account of where his school is in the Ofsted inspection cycle?

External accountability is important, but it is neither the beginning nor the end of leading a successful school. Values and the way in which they translate into the life of the school are at the centre of the work of successful schools and it is a vital part of the job of school leaders to ensure that values remain centre-stage, influencing every aspect of school life. Holding on to those values and, whatever pressures come from Ofsted or the government, using every opportunity to promote them, not only keep the school on a steadier course, but make the job of school leadership more doable and more enjoyable. This chapter emphasises the essential points that this approach brings professional control of the school's destiny and helps to avoid the feeling of being constantly reactive to government-imposed change.

Clarity of values and vision and the determination to put those values into practice and thus take control of the educational agenda in the school are at the heart of this book.

Co-operative trust schools

One group of schools very clear about being values-led is the co-operative schools group. These schools are co-ordinated by the Schools Co-operative Society (SCS), which has its values firmly rooted in the wider co-operative movement. These values are set out in the box below.[1]

Co-operative values

- **Self-help:** Encouraging all within the organisation to help each other, by working together to gain mutual benefits. Helping people to help themselves
- **Self-responsibility:** To take responsibility for, and answer to, our actions
- **Democracy:** To give our stakeholders a say in the way we run our school
- **Equality:** Equal rights and benefits according to their contribution
- **Equity:** Being fair and unbiased
- **Solidarity:** Supporting each other and those in other co-operatives

Co-operative ethical values

These are consistent with the values of the founders of the co-operative movement:

- **Openness**
- **Honesty**
- **Social responsibility**
- **Caring for others**

---

1   www.co-operativeschools.coop/about_us/values_and_principles/more_about_
     our_values_and_principles

The SCS website (www.co-operativeschools.coop) goes on to state that co-operative schools are about developing a balanced set of values that will help young people become the good citizens our society needs. These values are not confined to UK schools and are in use in co-operatives across the world.

The example of the SCS is a good place to start this discussion of values-led leadership because it shows how a group of schools has developed, not by being merged at gunpoint into a chain or an academy trust, but by school leaders and governors signing up to the values that are the driving force of the group.

Whether a school stands on its own or is part of a group, a values-led school is almost always a good school. Successful school leaders are open and clear about the values underpinning the work of the institution. Values are constantly reiterated to staff, students, parents and the wider community.

There is so much change in education and so many new (and renewed) policies to implement and demands to answer that it is all too easy for school leaders to lose focus. Part of the job of a good head is to act as a sieve and only let through to others those things that really matter. Having a clear set of values helps the head to do this and thus to maintain focus on what should always be the top priorities – putting the values of the school into everyday practice and pursuing high quality teaching and learning.

The values driving those who work in education seem to me to remain as strong as ever – perhaps stronger than they have ever been – as we seek to close the gaps between the achievements of young people from different backgrounds.

Wider political events in the world have caused the UK government to become involved in the debate about values in schools.

British values

In November 2014 the Department for Education (DfE) published guidance, which had first been set out by the government in 2011, on promoting British values in schools so young people leave school prepared for life in modern Britain.

The 2014 guidance placed a duty on schools to 'actively promote' the values of democracy, the rule of law, individual liberty, and mutual respect and tolerance of those with different faiths and beliefs, which the DfE describes as the 'fundamental British values', although many people would see these values as part of Western culture rather than specifically British. According to the schools minister, Lord Nash, this new duty on schools was designed to 'tighten up the standards on pupil welfare to improve safeguarding, and the standards on spiritual, moral, social and cultural development of pupils to strengthen the barriers to extremism'.

I recall a meeting in 2008, when I was ASCL general secretary, with the secretary of state, Ed Balls, and the permanent secretary, Sir David Bell, following a briefing they had had from the security services, when they asked a group of us to consider how schools could help to identify potential extremists at an early stage. Subsequent events in Brussels, Paris and elsewhere have raised the importance of this agenda. The schools' context was brought into the public eye in 2014 at the time of the so-called 'Trojan Horse' affair concerning the governing bodies of some Birmingham schools. So, as so often happens when a story gains momentum in the media, the government had to be seen to 'do something about it' and the minister, Lord Nash, spoke of the need for all schools to promote basic British values. Examples of the aims of this policy were that pupils are expected to acquire:[2]

- *'an understanding of how citizens can influence decision-making through the democratic process*
- *an understanding that the freedom to hold other faiths and beliefs is protected in law*
- *an acceptance that people having different faiths or beliefs from oneself (or having none) should be accepted and tolerated, and should not be the cause of prejudicial or discriminatory behaviour*
- *an understanding of the importance of identifying and combatting discrimination'*

This is noteworthy because it is the first time the government has set out values or placed a duty on schools to adopt them. What is far from unique is that the government has acted in a way that affects all schools in order to combat a problem in a small number of places. Ofsted has subsequently heavily criticised some faith schools that have not put these values into practice, while most schools have had to make only small changes because these 'British values' are incorporated within the wider set of values on which school aims and policies are built.

Indeed, schools where values are firmly established are unlikely to have waited for direction from the secretary of state or Ofsted on a matter at the heart of the ethos of the school. Nor would school value statements be confined to matters of faith, but would cover a much broader description of discrimination.

---

2   www.gov.uk/government/news/guidance-on-promoting-british-values-in-schools-published

The place of values in a school

Education brings benefits to both individuals and society and a school's values reflect both, as we have seen in the discussion above about British values being embedded in schools.

For individual young people, schools aim to support and influence their development as fulfilled citizens, in intellectual, spiritual, cultural, physical, social and economic terms.

This development needs to take place within the moral framework of a set of values. Without this, we can produce highly intelligent bigots or even mass murderers, such as Pol Pot, the Khmer Rouge leader in Cambodia, who won a scholarship to study at the Ecole Française de Radioélectricité in Paris for four years from 1949 – an extreme example of what can result when a highly intelligent young person does not have an over-riding moral compass.

Some schools have carried out a consultative process with staff, pupils, parents and the community about the values on which their work should be based. The additional work of organising the consultation and discussing the results before agreeing on the school's values increases the extent to which the agreed values become part of the everyday life of the school.

Typically, the values for individuals in the school community include honesty, respect for others, willingness to help others, and a sense of justice. A value statement for the school itself might well include equity, high expectations, opportunity, enjoyment, trust and the valuing of diversity, but there can be no off-the-peg version for a school's values, exportable from another school's website.

No two school statements of values will be the same, as they will be rooted in the context and history of the school. The different value statements of two outstanding schools illustrate this: Lampton School in multicultural West London and the 400-year-old Queen Elizabeth School, Kirkby Lonsdale, Cumbria are good examples of how context influences values.

Lampton School, Hounslow: Extract from the statement of vision and intent[3]

The Lampton School community values diversity and seeks to give everyone in the school an equal chance to learn, work and live, free from the action, or fear, of racism, discrimination, or prejudice. By our actions we will work together to develop the potential of all pupils academically, socially, culturally and psychologically and to establish a community that is just and fair for all people who work at or visit Lampton School.

Students will be happy and healthy, enthused by the intellectual, social and physical challenges posed by their experience at school. They will be independent learners, aware of how to learn and of the role of emotions and dispositions in the learning process, which they draw on to address challenge and difficulty, as well as success.

Lampton is a mixed, 11-18 comprehensive school which sees the rich cultural heritage as perhaps the most important of its many strengths. It is a truly international school.

We foster a genuine sense of respect for the individual alongside an appreciation of the cultures and beliefs of others.

Queen Elizabeth School, Kirkby Lonsdale, Cumbria: School website section on 'QES values' [4]

- Respecting the past and its traditions
- Working hard and doing your best
- Being decent to others
- Being polite, friendly, courteous
- Looking out for others
- Getting involved
- Respecting the environment
- Thinking of others less fortunate
- Encouraging global citizenship
- Remembering that life is about more than money and material things

---

3   www.lampton.org.uk/wp-content/uploads/2013/03/School-Mission-Statement-Ethos.pdf
4   moodle.queenelizabeth.cumbria.sch.uk/pluginfile.php/204638/mod_resource/content/1/QESSchoolValues2014-15.pdf

Faith schools attach a high degree of importance to setting out their values clearly. In the small village primary school where I was a governor for many years, the six principles of friendship, honesty, forgiveness, respect, kindness and dedication underpin the school's curriculum and its wider work. It is in the implementation of these values that the distinctly Christian ethos of the school comes through. The headteacher of St Andrew's, Heather White, says:

'We started by discussing what values were important to us as practitioners and Christians. We aimed to embed these values across everything – the curriculum, assemblies, the way we respond to each other, decisions we make. We also give certificates. Our values have over the last two years become so well embedded that many of the certificates we give out are a result of children coming to tell us where they have seen Christian values in others.

One of our key values is respect and I think through this value we cover such a lot of what is very important, understanding other cultures and how a multicultural society works.'

St Andrew's CE Primary School, North Kilworth, Leicestershire: Extract from the school's statement of aims and values[5]

The statement, which is in three sections, includes the following:

The achievement of high standards

- Encourage personal responsibility for behaviour
- Develop lively, enquiring minds and a sense of awe and wonder
- Develop children who aspire to reach their potential and are independent learners
- Ensure there is a safe, attractive and stimulating environment for the children

Development of good citizens

- Develop an understanding and tolerance of other races and faiths
- Develop positive and supportive relationships engendering sensitivity, empathy and respect
- Encourage children to feel part of the community and contribute to it Encourage respect for people, property and the environment

---

5   www.standrewsnorthkilworth.co.uk

Creation of enthusiastic, creative learners

- Provide opportunities for the development of an imaginative and questioning mind in all children
- Ensure children become independent, responsible and self-motivated individuals
- Encourage all children to identify and celebrate their successes

School value statements also sometimes include a determination to bring the benefits of high quality education to all in the area by working closely with other schools and doing nothing that is against their interests.

While a school's values are transmitted through carefully considered statements, school prospectuses and staff handbooks, they are most powerfully put into action through the minutiae of the school day. A headteacher who runs an extra-curricular club transmits the message to staff that this is an important part of school life. A head who checks a pupil for the way s/he talks to another pupil in a school corridor gives out a message about mutual respect that will be absorbed by all within hearing distance. Other heads emphasise different aspects of school life, such as advice to pupils on the way they should, or should not, enter classrooms, or by giving a cheery word of welcome to pupils when they arrive at school in the morning. Heads cannot do everything themselves; they must work though the staff team, so the best way to influence the life of the school is to ensure that others are set the example of how the school's values should be put into practice.

Revisiting a school's value statement periodically ensures not only that it can reflect changes in society and new pressures on young people, but that it is properly reflected in the daily life of the school. Revisiting values and discussing them openly is helpful in embedding values into all aspects of the work of a school.

First impressions matter

A school's values are visible in every aspect of its work. Tony Blair said that he could see if a school is good from the moment he walked in. Even allowing for the supernatural powers of a prime minister, there is both exaggeration and truth in this statement. First impressions really do matter.

One experienced headteacher told me the story of the first visit he and his wife paid to a large local hospital for her cancer tests – a nervous time for them both, to say the least. The first person they encountered was the hospital car park attendant who gave them directions to the relevant department and advised them 'I wouldn't come here if I were you'.

I went with my wife one Sunday morning for an exploratory visit to a school advertising a headship for which she was thinking of applying. These two doubtless suspicious-looking strangers brought the caretaker out of his house to see what we were doing and we explained to him why we were there. He was uncomplimentary about the departing head, comparing him unfavourably with the previous head, whom he praised for his strong disciplinary stance. The school did not come across well in this conversation.

I used to be a trustee of a charity that worked with stately homes and other places open to the public. Part of this work was the training of front-of-house staff, who learned from our charity about the '90:90 rule' – first-time visitors form 90 per cent of their view of a place in the first 90 seconds of their visit. This rule can apply to schools too. The appearance of a school's entrance and foyer, and the welcome visitors receive from the reception staff, are a critical part of the outward-facing reputation of the school.

Leading a values-led school

There are public occasions at which school leaders can ensure that the school's values shine through the spoken word – awards ceremonies, meetings for parents who are considering the school for their children, visits to local primary schools, early meetings for new pupils, meetings about courses in Key Stage 4 and the sixth form, and school assemblies.

Even more importantly, good leaders live their ideals and constantly put their values into practice as they go about the daily tasks of leadership. The way they talk to pupils as they move around the school; the way they enter classrooms when a lesson is taking place; the way they communicate orally and in writing with staff; what they do at breaktime, lunchtime and lesson changes; the shape of the agenda for staff meetings; the seating arrangement in the offices of senior staff – all these actions communicate the values of the institution and its leaders.

I strongly agree that 'school leaders need unwarranted optimism' as part of their DNA[6] and indeed 'Smile' was one of the ten lessons learned on my own leadership journey, included in my blog post.[7] If the leaders of the school walk around looking glum, there is little chance that teachers and other staff will

6   Tim Brighouse, 'The passionate teacher and the passionate leader in the passionate school', in Brent Davies and Tim Brighouse (eds.), Passionate leadership in education, Sage Publications, 2008. See below, chapter 8.

7   johndunfordconsulting.wordpress.com/2011/11/01/ten-things-learned-on-my-leadership-journey/

enjoy their work or convey to the pupils the joy of learning and a positive climate of success and aspiration. Teaching is for optimists and school leadership is for supreme optimists.

An important part of a values-led school is having staff who believe in those values, so having total commitment to them from staff is vital if vision is to be turned into reality in the lives of the young members of the school community.

This staff commitment starts with appointment procedures that convey the values of the school in the advertisement, job details and interview process. The reputation of a school, for better or worse, accurate or misleading, goes well beyond its physical location. Interviewees will arrive with preconceptions that may not be based in the reality of the school's situation. As a headteacher, I regarded the first hour of any interview day as vitally important in conveying to candidates the values of the school and our aspirations for its future. This sometimes resulted in candidates making an early withdrawal when they discovered the school and the job were not as they had imagined. So be it; we were better off without them.

The same thinking that goes into the design of the interview day can also underpin the induction process for the successful candidate, constantly reinforcing the values of the institution during the vital early months in the job.

This approach is needed for supply teachers too. New supply teachers do not have much time to learn about the school before they go into their first lesson, so it is important to have a very short booklet for supply teachers, setting out briefly the values of the school and agreed processes, such as how lessons should be started and ended and how to call for assistance in times of difficulty.

A booklet for teachers in training is equally important and, like the staff handbook, this should start with values and the way in which they are embedded in the school's teaching and learning policy.

Community values

Schools want to be part of their local community, although open enrolment has almost destroyed the link between some schools and their local community or between some secondary schools and what used to be termed their 'feeder' primary schools, with 11 year olds now coming from as many as 70 different primary schools into some secondaries.

Community values may be difficult for a school to discern, since most schools will not have a homogeneous intake. Where there is a degree of homogeneity, however, the values of the local community may not be ones that the school would wish to adopt. I have worked in schools where the predominant local culture is one of high aspiration for young people, a climate that makes the job of the school considerably easier, but I have also worked in places where many parents have low expectations and where the school, if it is to be successful, needs to work within the local community to communicate its values and raise the aspirations and expectations of what the young people can achieve.

In 2013, the secretary of state, Michael Gove, talked about the 'smell of defeatism' in schools in East Durham – unwisely, as it transpired that he had visited no schools in East Durham and the quote was based on a statement ten years earlier by a teacher in a school in Sunderland, a city that has been independent from Durham County Council since 1888.

East Durham is typified by Easington, where the miners' strike in 1984 had a profound effect on the local community, as seen in the film *Billy Elliot,* much of which was set in the streets of this small mining town. The secondary school in the town had a difficult job to do, particularly in the aftermath of the closure of the coal mine in 1993, with little local employment available to school leavers. In 2015 I had the privilege of visiting the successor school, Easington Academy, which was the winner of the north-east regional pupil premium award that year. The headteacher, Toni Spoors, who had been a pupil in the sixth form at Durham Johnston School when I was head there, is constantly reinforcing the school's values of high aspiration and high-quality teaching and learning in ways that illustrate just how wrong Michael Gove's remark was. Easington is a school that is fully engaged in, and leading, its local community.

Another school that is leading its community is Northampton Academy, which I visited soon after it opened. Northampton secondary schools had a tough time in the 2000s, with many low-grade Ofsted judgements, and Northampton Academy was one of the first in the area to be allocated to a sponsor, United Learning. It would have been easy for the new school, in a superb new building, to have established its reputation by attracting bright pupils from other parts of the town and its surrounding area, but the school chose to focus on its immediate community, where there was a history of low aspiration and poor educational attainment. Unsurprisingly in such a school, the community is very much part of the school values and ethos, as stated in the United Learning statement on the school website:[8]

'The best schools are underpinned by an ethos, behaviour and tradition that are understood, respected and valued by everyone across the school community.

That is why we place a great emphasis on being a values-led organisation with an ethos established to bring hope and aspiration to the communities we serve in

---

8   www.northampton-academy.org/AboutUs/EthosandValues.aspx

our schools. Our values act as a yardstick for how we behave, interact with each other and deliver our mission.

During the first half of 2012, our staff, students and governors were consulted on refreshing our values; to identify the concepts, attributes and behaviours that exemplify what it genuinely means to bring out the best in everyone.

The consensus across the group was that our ethos is best articulated through the following: Ambition, Confidence, Determination, Creativity, Respect, and Enthusiasm.

You will see these attributes brought to life in our school through how we engage with each other and our community, how we behave and how we inspire ourselves and each other.'

As with the values of SCS schools, this illustrates how groups of schools are increasingly adopting shared values.

The tradition of state schools in England, like their independent cousins, is that they have many freedoms they can exercise, such as the way in which they engage with their local community, how they teach and assess, what extra-curricular activities they offer, and especially what values underpin their work.

Yet many headteachers feel constrained to follow the line taken by the government and Ofsted, a situation that can be explained only in the context of an over-bearing accountability system and too much direction from central government. Professor John Hattie powerfully reminds us that there are too many distractions for school leaders from what is important in leading good schools and successful learning.[9] Government documents for schools are full of words like 'deliver' and 'performance' and have little or no mention of the fundamental concepts of understanding and personal development, which school aims and values generally prioritise.

There are those who saw the 'Every Child Matters' (ECM) agenda in the mid-2000s as a potential distraction from the standards agenda, which had been the main driver of government policy since 1997.[10] True, it placed many additional burdens on schools, but it also emphasised the need both to safeguard children and to ensure that all school policies supported the needs of children from more deprived backgrounds. In those senses, it reinforced the values of schools to educate and develop all children to the full. For schools, every child really

---

9   John Hattie, What doesn't work in education: the politics of distraction, Pearson, 2015; www.pearson.com/content/dam/corporate/global/pearson-dot-com/files/hattie/150602_DistractionWEB_V2.pdf

10   See John Bangs, John Macbeath and Maurice Galton, Reinventing schools, reforming teaching, Routledge, 2011, pp.40-44

does matter and it is through the enactment of the school values that this is prioritised.

An ambiguous message was sent out when, on becoming secretary of state in 2010, Michael Gove abolished all mentions of 'Every Child Matters' by his staff, as well as removing the ECM logos that had sprung up on every wall and lift in the DfE during the time of Ed Balls as secretary of state.

Rights respecting schools

It was through Michael Gove's request to me in 2010 to review the Office of the Children's Commissioner (OCC) that I became familiar with the UNICEF Rights Respecting Schools award, now held by over 4000 schools in the UK. These schools have a very clear set of values, based on the rights of the child.

Shortly after the 2010 general election, a bonfire of quangos took place, with Michael Gove taking apparent delight in leading the purge demanded by the Cabinet Office. The Qualifications and Curriculum Development Agency (QCDA), the School Food Trust and the British Educational Communications and Technology Agency (BECTA) all disappeared, with varied degrees of mourning. The OCC could well have been added to this list, but Gove's zeal was held in check by the Liberal Democrat coalition partners, and in particular Nick Clegg, who dug in their collective toes and refused to sanction the abolition of the OCC, which became the only quango on which an inquiry was held to decide its future. I was asked to conduct the inquiry and was given a team of three civil servants to support me. No one leant on me and I was given a free hand in how I conducted the inquiry.

The OCC had made little impact since its foundation in the 2004 Children Act. This was less the fault of the first two children's commissioners, the former children's surgeon Sir Al Aynsley-Green and the ex-director of Gateshead children's services Maggie Atkinson, than of the weakness of the legislation. Tony Blair had been frightened to include specific reference to children's rights in the law of the land and so the Act stated that the role of the commissioner was to look after the views and interests of children in relation to the five outcomes of Every Child Matters. I was under no illusion that the Conservative wing of the government, and Michael Gove in particular, would similarly be chary about statutorily giving children their rights. When I mooted the idea privately to politicians that I should recommend that the role of the commissioner be strengthened to state that s/he should 'protect the rights of children under the UN Convention on the Rights of the Child', a Liberal Democrat peer said to me: '*You will never get away with that.*' But I did. Graham Stuart, the excellent chair of the House of Commons Select Committee on Education at the time, had reinforced my determination to make a radical recommendation by telling me I should recommend either abolishing the OCC or giving it a proper role. And a proper role meant that, like the children's commissioners in Ireland and the other three countries of the UK, the work of the children's commissioner in England should be focused on the UK's position as a signatory to the UN Convention. With only the USA (which leaves the decision to individual states) and Somalia as non-signatories, I could hardly have suggested taking England out of its responsibilities as a signatory. The recommendations of my report were accepted by the secretary of state and incorporated into the Children and Families Act 2014.[11]

Perhaps Michael Gove was happy to concede this victory to the Liberal Democrats because he did not regard the OCC as particularly important and its retention would give him a good bargaining counter for the battles he wanted to fight with his coalition partners on what he regarded as more significant issues. Gove was a strong supporter of the coalition in its first two years, when the Liberal Democrat education minister was the highly committed but relatively weak Sarah Teather. When David Laws took her place in 2013 (by which time Nick Clegg had had a very public falling out with Gove), battles were engaged more frequently between the LibDems and the secretary of state.

I am sure Michael Gove's acceptance of my recommendations, and their subsequent inclusion in statute, was helped by the paragraphs on rights respecting schools, which pointed out that the emphasis on children's rights is matched by an emphasis on the exercise of responsibilities and respect for others. The values of rights respecting schools make clear that they are consciously producing good citizens. Children in these schools learn about their own rights and, in doing so, have a greater appreciation of the need to respect the rights of others. Research by the University of Sussex found that teaching children about their rights can reduce exclusions and bullying, improve teacher-pupil relationships, raise attainment and make for more mature and responsible students. Once parents have understood the principles of rights respecting schools, this can also improve the relationship between school and home.[12]

***

Whether a good school is part of the Schools Co-operative Society, an academy group, a multi-academy trust, a faith school, a rights-respecting school, or

---

11   John Dunford, Review of the Office of the Children's Commissioner (England), HMSO Cmnd 7981, 2010, www.gov.uk/government/publications/review-of-the-office-of-the-childrens-commissioner-england; www.legislation.gov.uk/ukpga/2014/6/contents/enacted

12   Dunford, ibid, p.24

whether it stands alone, values are likely to be at the centre of its policies and these will be clearly articulated both in the daily life of the school and on set-piece occasions. Revisiting value statements and reviewing them helps to reinforce the extent to which they are embedded in everyday practice. In schools that are clear about their values, these underpin teaching and learning in lessons and behaviour at all times, as well as the way in which the school interacts with other schools. Values should always be at the heart of school leadership.

Chapter 2

Navigating a route for the school

There will be a focus on standards, not structures.
Rt Hon David Blunkett MP,
Secretary of State for Education, 1997

An emphasis on structures

Introducing the new Labour government's education White Paper, Excellence in Schools,[1] soon after the 1997 general election, David Blunkett spoke the words, quoted above, that he undoubtedly wanted to define his years as secretary of state. Yet even he could not resist the temptation for all education secretaries of state to tinker with the structure of the school system.

Primary schools have been largely immune from this maelstrom of structural legislation, with few becoming grant-maintained schools in the 1990s, although a steadily growing percentage of primary schools are now becoming academies, with encouragement to work together within multi-academy trusts. For primary school leaders, there has also been a large amount of change to deal with, local management of schools and the development of school business management being a big challenge in a small school with little leadership capacity. Primary schools in many areas have also seen a significant decrease in the support available to them from their local authority, on which they had traditionally drawn considerably.

---

1   www.educationengland.org.uk/documents/wp1997/excellence-in-schools.html

It is secondary schools that have borne the main consequences of government ministers finding it easier to make a newspaper headline with a structural change than with an announcement about school standards. However, from about 2012, the government has increasingly driven change through reform of examinations, qualifications and accountability measures, rather than directly addressing standards, as David Blunkett attempted with the literacy and numeracy initiatives.

While primary schools have continued to serve all the children of a local community, secondary schools have been faced with a bewildering array of different types of school. Since the mid-1990s, state-funded secondary schools have been able to be:

1. Comprehensive schools

2. Secondary modern schools

3. Grammar schools

4. Faith schools (voluntary-aided or voluntary-controlled)

5. Community schools

6. Foundation schools

7. Specialist schools (with a choice of ten specialisms)

8. City technology colleges (CTCs)

9. Grant-maintained schools

10. Beacon schools

11. Studio schools

12. University technical colleges

13. Academies (sponsored or convertor)

14. Trust schools

15. Free schools

16. Teaching schools

17. National support schools

18. State boarding schools

19. Special schools

In the early 1990s, I had to give a talk about the English education system to a group of Japanese people, who are accustomed to their countrywide network of local community schools, with children spending six years at elementary school, three years at junior high school, three years at senior high school, and two or four years at university. Although only seven of the 19 types of school in England mentioned above existed then, the explanation of schooling in England is further complicated by the fact that children can change from one phase to another at 8, 9, 10, 11, 12, 13 and 14 in different parts of the country. I do not envy anyone charged with giving a clear description of the structure of schools in England in the 21st century, nor any foreigner trying to understand it. My Japanese audience could see no logic in it. In short, it is incomprehensible, and countless hours have been wasted by governing boards and school leadership teams in trying to navigate a path through it.

The purpose of this chapter is to offer some assistance to those who wish to do so while maintaining their school's values.

The volume of reform

I joined a school leadership team in January 1974 as one of a new breed of 'senior teachers', the equivalent to assistant heads. Margaret Thatcher was coming to the end of her four years as secretary of state for education, since when there have been 19 secretaries of state serving for an average of 2.2 years, over 35 Education Acts, and numerous regulations and reports that also had an impact on schools, including health and safety legislation and child safeguarding laws and regulations. As some changes have come in, other rules have been scrapped.

Part of the problem is that the 24-hour media report ministers in action, not sitting at their desks, so the media drive a situation in which governments tend to be judged by the quantity of their actions, rather than the effectiveness of policies that, in the case of education, may well not make a difference until after the next general election. So ministers feel bound to respond to media stories, publicising their policies through visits to schools that do not need visiting, meeting people who later appear on government committees, and garnering ideas that are sometimes later imposed on all schools. Civil servants suggest new ways in which ministers' perceived wishes might be furthered in practice. Announcements are made in order to achieve soon forgotten headlines, which leave schools with initiatives that may take years to implement fully.

After nearly two years as secretary of state, Michael Gove told the ASCL annual conference in March 2012: '*Lest anyone think we have reached a point where we should slacken the pace of reform, let me reassure them – we have to accelerate.*' The *Times Educational Supplement* reported that the school leaders at the conference '*politely but firmly made their displeasure known*', with the ASCL general secretary, Brian Lightman, saying that '*by accelerating the reform too much, you prevent us from doing it properly.*' Michael Gove's response at the press conference after his speech was that, *'If people say it's all a bit too much, then my view is "man up".* If you allow an evidence-based, pragmatically-arrived-at programme of change, which is driven by a desire for social justice, to be derailed by people saying that change is too fast then, as Martin Luther King pointed out, you end up being an ally of the forces of stagnation.' [2]

These are the words of a man on a mission, rather than a politician who wanted to evaluate the evidence and work with the profession.

Andrew Adonis[3] is a supporter of the view that reform cannot wait for evidence. In his book on school reform, he states that the development of academies had to take place before the evidence was available on their success and was frustrated by education department ministers and officials in his desire to expand the academies programme at high speed.[4]

There is no single date each year for introducing new laws or changes in procedure. Changes come in at different times of year, which makes the process of implementation more difficult for school leaders and can be disruptive for learners, as was the case with Michael Gove's announcement of an EBacc accountability measure after the 2012-13 academic year had started.

The extent of the regulatory burden on schools was investigated by the House of Lords Merits Committee in 2009. The report, *The cumulative impact of statutory instruments on schools,*[5] stated that in 2006-07 there had been 100 new regulations placed on schools by the government, with the education department and its national agencies producing over 760 documents aimed at schools in that year. The report stated: *'No single part of the department was aware of the totality of what was being offered.'* The department did not review the effect of new regulations and so did not know whether policy objectives had been achieved. The report proposed that the department should act as a gatekeeper to shield schools from burdens imposed by other government departments, and said all regulations should be published by April to give schools a term's notice before having to implement them at the beginning of the academic year in September.

The report considered that the department should take a 'less heavy-handed' approach to maintained schools and reflected on the difference between

---

2   Times Educational Supplement, 30 March 2012

3   Andrew Adonis was the prime minister's adviser on education from 1998 to 2005, when he became Lord Adonis and worked as a schools minister until 2008.

4   Education, education, education: reforming England's schools, Biteback, 2012

5   House of Lords Merits of Statutory Instruments Committee, The cumulative impact of statutory instruments on schools, 9th Report of Session 2008-09, HMSO 2009

intention and reality: '*If the department considers that the light-touch regulatory framework for academies is appropriate and successful, that lighter touch should be extended to all maintained schools.*'

The committee chair, Lord Filkin, whose background was as a local authority chief executive and junior education minister, said: '*The committee has concluded that able, brilliant and skilled professionals do not thrive when their energies are absorbed by the need to comply with a raft of detailed requirements. If the government makes the broad objectives clear, practitioners should be given the freedom to deliver using their own skill and experience, without the need for wide-ranging prescription. We call on the department to shift its primary focus away from the regulation of processes through statutory instruments, towards establishing accountability for the delivery of key outcomes.*'

As general secretary of ASCL, I responded to the House of Lords Merits Committee report by saying that, in 2008, schools in England were besieged by 79 policy consultations and at least 300 announcements from the government and that we were expecting even more in 2009. I was quoted in the *Guardian* as warmly welcoming the report: '*We have a deficit model of policy making, with school and college leaders not trusted and the government always assuming that schools are doing things badly. I sometimes think that the purpose that drives the government is its belief in the power of legislation ... The juggernaut of policies, laws and regulations hurtles at ever increasing speed towards us, seemingly out of control. There is just too much policy, too quickly introduced. I like the example set by the slow food movement. Let me make a plea for slow policy – wholemeal, organic, evidence-based, widely consulted, consensus policies that are introduced one at a time, properly evaluated and put on the compost heap when they go off.*' [6]

The burden falls particularly heavily on governing boards, whose part-time role has very high expectations laid upon them by the government. Indeed, the department's own guidance to governors runs to 114 pages[7] and does not include a full list of the responsibilities of governing boards. When I requested in 2009 that the department produce such a summary, I recall that their final version had some notable omissions. This was somewhat alarming, although perhaps not surprising when one considers that the responsibilities of school governors originate from at least 100 pieces of legislation, including the Companies Act 1985, the Disability Discrimination Act 1995, the Freedom of Information Act 2000, the Health and Safety at Work Act 1974, and the Sex Discrimination Act

---

6   Guardian, 13 March 2009, /www.theguardian.com/education/2009/mar/13/lords-report-dcsf

7   Governance handbook, HMSO, 2015

1975 (as amended by the Equality Act 2006). Every new Education Act adds to the list of governors' responsibilities. Governing boards are also required by law to have policies on around 30 different matters, such as teachers' pay, the school curriculum, charging and remissions, and pupil discipline.

As we saw in chapter 1, the amount of government activity, placing such burdens on school leaders and governing boards, has the capacity to distract them from the main thrust of their work. As Professor John Hattie says:

'The evidence shows that what's most important [for school leaders] is to focus on the classroom – that is, championing teacher expertise, and spreading it from classroom to classroom. Yet, too often, policymakers propose school-wide solutions that have little proven effect, such as lengthening the school day or year, or creating new forms of schools, which tend not to be any better than existing options.

It is ironic that a popular solution to claims about "failing schools" is to invent new forms of schools. There is a remarkable hunger to create charter schools, for-profit schools, lighthouse schools, free schools, academies, public-private schools – anything other than a public school. But, given that the variance in student achievement between schools is small relative to variance within schools, it is folly to believe that a solution lies in different forms of schools.

These new forms of schools usually start with a fanfare, with self-selected staff (and sometimes selected students) and are sought by parents who want "something better". Indeed, there is evidence there is a slight increase in achievement in these schools in the short-term, but the long-term effects lead to no differences when compared with public schools. The effect of charter schools, for example, across three meta-analyses based on 246 studies, is a minuscule .07.

This lack of a marked effect is surely not surprising when it is realised that within a year or so the "different" school becomes just another school, with all the usual issues that confront all schools.' [8]

Leading a school with autonomy

One of the beliefs cited as a distraction by Hattie is an increase in autonomy, a policy actively pursued in England since 1988, when Kenneth Baker piloted the Education Reform Act through Parliament, bringing in local management of schools (LMS) and grant-maintained (GM) schools. There is a fuller discussion of how autonomy impacts on school leadership in chapter 8, but the direction since 1988 of much government policy on school structures has been to create

---

8   John Hattie, What doesn't work in education: the politics of distraction, Pearson, 2015, p.23

schools with greater autonomy from local authorities, such as city technology colleges (CTCs), academies and free schools.

Hattie states that his reading of the international evidence on school autonomy is that:

'achievement is higher in countries where schools have autonomy in staffing decisions, in hiring teachers and where there are high levels of external accountability (such as inspections and external exit examinations), but negative when schools have autonomy over formulating their own budget.'

But he points out that:

'the debate about school autonomy misses two major issues. First, the greater the amount of local autonomy, the more likely it is that schools become unequal: the better schools tend to become better, and the not-so-good schools tend to become worse. Second, granting autonomy to schools and principals distracts from the real issue: to what level should individual teachers have autonomy over how they teach?' [9]

Because of the volume of legislation and change to state education in England, it is extremely difficult to isolate the impact of specific factors, such as autonomy, so it will be some years before a definitive verdict can be given on the success or failure of schools with greater autonomy from local authorities. Because so much is controlled centrally by the government and the constraints created by the accountability system are a massive influence, many school leaders do not feel as autonomous as the rhetoric of government ministers would like the public to believe. However, as we shall see in later chapters, there are many different ways in which this autonomy can be used, not all of them beneficial to the system as a whole, so it is incumbent on school leaders to consider how they can use the freedoms they have, both for the good of the young people in their school and for the health and success of the wider system.

Jon Coles, formerly director-general of schools in the Department for Education (DfE) and now chief executive of a large academy chain, has written that he was often surprised, when in government, by the 'over-compliance' of schools to the announced policies of the DfE[10] and I share his view that schools have a lot more space to do what they feel needs to be done than they realise.

---

9   Ibid, p.24
10   Times Educational Supplement, 21 June 2013

Local authorities squeezed from above and below

The biggest side effect of the policy thrust towards more autonomous schools has been the disempowerment of local education authorities. Indeed, the acronym, LEA, for so long at the core of policy development and dissemination in England, has disappeared and the education role of the local authority has been reduced by the increase in school autonomy and, even more, by a massive increase in the powers that central government has given itself.

Since the 1980s, however, central governments have been far more certain about the alleged shortcomings of local authorities in education than about how they should replace them. Consequently, a gaping hole has appeared in many parts of the country between central government and individual schools, with the 'missing middle' being filled partly by academy chain sponsors, partly by increasing the powers of regional school commissioners, and partly by teaching schools. The most contested part of the local authority's education role is school improvement and this is discussed in chapter 9.

The 2016 White Paper set out a new role for local authorities. If implemented, this could bring some much needed clarity to the role, so it is unfortunate that it is based on the oft-repeated calumny that 'local authorities run schools', which they have not done since at least 1988.

In the short term, the White Paper[11] states, '*local authorities will continue to have responsibilities which include: employment of staff in community schools; ownership and asset management of school buildings; and responsibilities relating to the governance, organisation and curriculum of maintained schools.*'

When all schools in an area become academies, these responsibilities will pass to the schools, and local authorities will be left with three residual areas of responsibility: ensuring that every child has a school place, ensuring that the needs of vulnerable pupils are met, and acting as champions for all parents and families. However, with the political turmoil that followed the European Union (EU) referendum and a new secretary of state, Justine Greening, appointed in Prime Minister Theresa May's first cabinet, the future of the White Paper, and hence of local authorities, remains uncertain.

The growth of academies

The powers of the local authority have dwindled in an incoherent way over a 30-year period and each phase of reform has presented a different set of questions for head teachers and governing boards.

---

11   www.education.gov.uk/government/publications/education-excellence-everywhere

The Education Reform Act of 1988 introduced LMS for all schools and GM status for the smaller number of schools wanting to work fully outside the local authority. The former was arguably the biggest reform to school management and the biggest difference to the work of school leaders since the Education Act of 1944. The latter was the forerunner of academy status.

Schools had to hold a ballot of parents in order to apply for GM status. As GM schools, they could use different admissions criteria from other local schools, introduce partial or whole selection by examination or interview, increase their admissions number, alter their age range or start a sixth form. Perhaps the greatest benefit of GM status was the ability to apply for capital building grants, an opportunity that the early converters to GM status were quick to grasp. With improved and extended buildings and around 10 per cent higher revenue funding each year, the cumulative effect of GM status over the 10 years of the scheme was considerable and few tears were shed by non-GM schools when, on the abolition of GM status in 1998, GM schools complained that the consequent cuts (of as much as £250,000 in the case of the Oratory School, which was attended by Tony Blair's sons), as they reverted to the funding level of LA-maintained schools, were causing hardship.[12]

Additional capital and revenue, ministerial visits, mentions in speeches and honours[13] had been bestowed on GM schools, reinforcing the view that this was the way to success, although inspectors found that GM status did not make an impact on the quality of teaching.[14] In short, GM schools enjoyed their independence, but many wasted the opportunities it presented and did not improve their outcomes.

Heads and governing bodies had to weigh the financial advantages of GM status against other factors, such as the damage to the local family of schools, where wounds from the GM era still exist in some places. In some parts of the country, such as Kent and Essex, a large number of secondary schools became GM, and this created an over-competitive climate, with GM heads not being invited to local heads' groups and some schools seeking to prosper at the expense of others. Under these circumstances, the number of GM schools was sometimes increased by schools seeking GM status for defensive reasons, seeing it as the only way that they could compete on a level playing field in their locality.

---

12   The Labour government gave GM schools an additional 2.5 per cent of revenue funding to compensate for this loss.

13   The highest honour for a headteacher during this period was an OBE and almost all the awards between 1988 and 1997 was made to heads of GM schools.

14   Ofsted, Grant maintained schools 1989-92, HMSO, 1993

Some schools also used GM status as a way of escaping a local reorganisation. In Kettering, for example, a single-sex boys' school (the former boys' grammar school, subsequently a weak comprehensive) had seen a fall in pupil numbers and was closed by the LA. The counterpart of the boys' school, Southfield School for Girls, then became the only single-sex school in the town and avoided the LA's closure plan by becoming GM.

GM status certainly was not for me or for the governors of Durham Johnston Comprehensive School. There was a climate of collaboration among schools in County Durham and an equally strong sense of social mission among the heads that we were there to improve the life chances of all the young people in the area, many of whom would have gone down the pit in previous generations.

By the time of the abolition of GM schools by the new Labour government in the School Standards and Framework Act of 1998, nearly one-fifth of secondary schools had become GM, which had a significant impact on the capacity of some local authorities to influence the course of secondary education in their areas. (See Table 2.1 below) The impact was particularly felt on school places and school admissions, which became extremely stressful for schools and especially for parents in areas such as Bromley, where 12 out of 13 secondary schools were GM.

	Grant maintained	LA maintained	Total
Primary	508 (2.8%)	17804	18312
Secondary	667 (18.7%)	2900	3567
Special	21 (1.3%)	1143	1164
Total	1196 (5.2%)	21847	23043

Table 2.1: Number of grant-maintained schools in England and Wales, 1998

Although the genesis of academies was in GM policy, the result of academy expansion has been both greater and rather different from the GM era. These two types of 'independent state schools', as Tony Blair liked to call them, had a similar birth, but a very different upbringing.

Following some spectacular failures to turn around challenging city schools under a 'fresh start' scheme, the initial phase of academies grew from the determination of the Labour government in the early 2000s to improve comprehensive schools with very poor examination results to which the urban middle class (including Tony Blair and his education adviser, Andrew Adonis) would not send their children. City technology colleges, on the other hand, were doing well in tough areas under sponsors such as the Mercers' Company, Lord

Harris the carpet magnate, and Peter Vardy the north-eastern car dealer.

Too many schools were in a cycle of decline and Adonis's scheme to break into the cycle was to expand this sponsorship idea, closing schools in trouble and re-opening them as independent academies, sponsored by business people such as Frank Lowe in Wembley, Harry Djanogly in Nottingham, Lord Harris and, most spectacularly, Clive Bourne, whose sponsorship in East London saw the notorious Hackney Downs School turned into the highly successful Mossbourne Academy. Through Ewan Harper, the Church of England sponsored several academies under the aegis of the United Learning Trust. Schools such as Thomas Telford City Technology College also became sponsors of other schools.

Uniquely, the driving force behind the implementation and expansion of academies was 10 Downing Street, not the DfE. I do not recall any other example of the prime minister's policy adviser taking this kind of responsibility for policy implementation on the ground. Feathers were certainly ruffled in the department, as Andrew Adonis recounts in his book.[15] His main ally in the department was the former Northamptonshire headteacher, Sir Bruce Liddington, with whom I recall a conversation on the pavement in Great Smith Street, just along from the DfE. Bruce was on his way from the DfE to Downing Street and I asked him about progress with the academy expansion project. What sticks in my mind about his reply is that he clearly believed – and I am sure it was true – that he was doing the prime minister's personal work, seeking additional sponsors and fixing meetings for them with Tony Blair to help to persuade them both to put up the money required at the time[16] and place their reputations at risk by publicly supporting the turning around of extremely challenging schools. Tony Blair was very persuasive in such conversations and, no doubt flattered by prime ministerial patronage, the number of sponsors grew quite rapidly.

After the 2005 general election, Andrew Adonis continued his detailed personal leadership of the academies programme, but as a junior education minister instead of Number 10 adviser, and by 2006, 200 sponsored academies were in the pipeline, most of which were fully functioning by the end of the Labour government in 2010.

The move from local authority to sponsor provided great opportunities for school leaders to take on the immense challenge of making these schools successful, but it was not such good news for the existing headteachers, who

---

15   Op.cit., 2012

16   This financial commitment was later fudged and then dropped.

rarely survived the transition to the new status. Football manager syndrome had begun for heads and my speeches to ASCL annual conferences charted the steady increase in the number of school leaders losing their jobs.

After the 2010 election the opportunity opened up for successful schools – those graded outstanding (and later, good) by Ofsted – to choose to become academies. These 'convertor' academies are independent state schools, owned by an academy trust, and do not have to follow the national curriculum, national agreements on teachers' pay and conditions, or the length of the teaching day or year, nor do their teachers have to be qualified. Instead, they are subject to a funding agreement with the secretary of state, meaning they have substituted a high degree of central government control for what in practice was a pretty light measure of control by local government.

With regional schools commissioners (RSCs) now being the eyes and ear of the DfE, academy heads and governors are subject to direct influence from central government and the notion of independent state schools has become a mixed blessing. As head of an LA-maintained school in County Durham in the 1980s and 1990s, I probably had more independence after LMS than heads of academies have under the watchful eyes of the DfE and its RSCs.

When school leaders and governors are weighing up the benefits and disadvantages of converting to academy status, they now see that the financial incentives that existed for early convertors in 2010-11 are no longer there; that there are both advantages and disadvantages in not being subject to national teachers' pay and conditions; and that there are arguments for and against the trust model of governance. There are other local issues to consider too, such as the status of schools with which there is a working partnership. In considering academy status, schools also recognise that academies have a different kind of relationship with the local authority, but a relationship does still exist.

By May 2016, over 60 per cent of secondary schools, many of which already felt distant from the local authority, had converted to academy status and the opportunity to do this as a group of schools forming a multi-academy trust, has encouraged some that would not otherwise have converted. A smaller proportion of primary schools has converted, but this is increasing as small primary schools recognise the diminishing support from local authorities and the advantages of working in multi-academy trusts. In total, there were 5302 academies in England in May 2016 – 29 per cent of all schools.

Phase of education	Converter	Sponsored	Percent	Total
Primary (incl. middle deemed primary)	2,079	967	18	3,046
Secondary (incl. middle deemed secondary, all through and 16+)	1,428	595	63	2,023
Special	147	31	19	178
Alternative Provision	42	13	14	55
Total	**3,696**	**1,606**	**29**	**5,302**

Table 2.2: Number of academies in England, May 2016 (Department for Education)

Some schools have considered what is on offer and decided to remain as LA-maintained, even though the level of service they receive from their LA may well have diminished as resources have contracted.

Geoff Barton, head of King Edward VI School, Bury St Edmunds, explains why his school has not become an academy:

'In May 2010, specialist status was quickly abandoned by the government as a unifying reform model. The government injected a level of divisiveness between schools that we found distasteful – in particular the (misguided) notion that schools that were 'outstanding' in Ofsted terms could apply to become academies. The cash incentives in that early phase also struck me as a dubious use of public money. The requirement for outreach work and partnership was a tokenistic footnote in the academy programme, and many heads reported a new and sour mood of competition – with neighbouring heads sometimes trying to poach students and teachers.

I watched as the school system appeared to splinter, and found the rhetoric of increased autonomy for headteachers unconvincing.

As a school we decided to stick with our principles, focusing on teaching and learning, not flirting with business models or appointing boards of trustees. And I think we have been vindicated in our decision. I suspect as headteacher of a local authority school I continue to enjoy more freedom than an academy head. So long as we continue to do well, the authority trusts me to lead the school. Stories from colleagues across England tell me that they feel hectored by their Regional Schools Commissioner, pressured to take on more schools and form multi-academy trusts.

It may, of course, be that our trajectory as a school is inevitable and that academisation lies ahead. But I hope it's not on my watch. Because I frequently remind myself of Churchill's stricture that (in his terms) England's headmasters enjoy more power than the prime minister. I came into the job to serve my students, parents and governors, not to implement an ideological government agenda based on a thin evidence base garnered via policy tourism.

I therefore couldn't be prouder that as the tectonic plates of educational structures have moved all around us, we have stuck true to our sense of distinctiveness as a school and seen our results continue to improve, our popularity with parents grow, and our sense of being the school we want to be get richer and deeper.'

Starting from the same point as Geoff Barton in wanting to develop the school from a set of thoroughly considered and well-established principles, Chris Clarke came to the opposite view and Queen Elizabeth School (QES), Kirkby Lonsdale in Cumbria, made an early application for academy status in 2010. Chris writes:

'Independence feels a natural state for the school. 425 years of history have built secure foundations, bred a feeling of confidence and reinforced a sense of security that all eventualities can be managed, all difficulties overcome. In addition, the school's position in a thriving, prosperous, well-connected, outward-looking market town and located on a three-county border with pupils attending from each county, helps promote a distinctive and unique character. Carlisle, the county town of the heterogeneous Cumbria is over an hour away and seems socially, culturally and economically far removed. Even before financial considerations or the notion of exploiting 'freedoms', becoming an academy seemed part of a natural evolution, an expression of a mature governing body's keenness to have mastery over its affairs and control its own destiny. Academisation was presented to staff, pupils and the wider community as an opportunity for the school to be 'more itself' rather than as a means of transformation.

Indeed, being 'more itself' is exactly how QES has responded to life as an academy. Fortunate and successful enough to have been able to evade the constraining effects and omnipresent surveillance of the accountability strictures (most particularly Ofsted inspections) the school has been in a position to articulate its philosophy with increasing confidence. Constantly redefining in a 21st century context the twin dimensions of 'scholarship and care', which date back to the school's original charter, QES has been able to champion a distinctive 'values education' centred around the ten explicit 'QES values'. [17] Of course, the school didn't need to have been an academy to develop this philosophy and indeed this ethos has been gestating for many years, but somehow 'independence' does seem to have encouraged the robust articulation of an 'identity'.

The 'freedoms' of the last few years have been less to do with academy status as such and more as a result of being successful enough to be trusted within the

---

17   See above, chapter 1, page 18

system to get on with things in our own way. Often, we have found ourselves at odds with government policy and intent upon finding creative solutions to developing teaching and learning, the curriculum and the pastoral system in ways which seem to be in the best interests of our pupils rather than because they tick the latest Ofsted box or yield to the latest DfE or ministerial fad. Governors value the sense of being in control of their own destiny, even if budgets make this more of a feeling than a reality, and academy status has given QES the wherewithal to put in place a succession plan, under which governors have identified publicly the next two QES headteachers, thereby explicitly articulating their determination to maintain the QES philosophy and ethos.'

As in the GM era, academy status has been used by some schools to maintain an age range that was about to disappear under LA reorganisation. This has happened with some middle school academies in Bedfordshire remaining in existence and thus obstructing the county's move to a two-tier system.

The autonomy of academy status has also been used to make a unilateral change to the age range of a school, leaving other local schools running to catch up in order to ensure their survival. In the 1970s Leicestershire earned national recognition for its reorganisation of secondary education into 11-14 high schools (although some were 10-14) and 14-19 community colleges. With academy status, some high schools decided unilaterally to change to an 11-16 age range, forcing other local high schools to consider the same decision and the local 14-19 community colleges to move to 11-19. With the LA powerless to act, the result for parents in Leicestershire is, at best, a very confused situation and, at worst, an extended period in which secondary education in the county will be in a state of flux.

The Gove era could be described as one of creative chaos, in which abolition and reform took place without a clear idea of the shape of the new system. Thus the General Teaching Council (GTC) was abolished without a plan for its roles, including teacher discipline, to be fulfilled; examinations were reformed without a coherent plan for the new system; schools were encouraged to become academies piecemeal, without a clear vision of the roles of central and local government in relation to the individual school. It may be, however, that the creative chaos of that period will become less chaotic as more and more schools form multi-academy trusts (MATs).

However, single academy trusts have been allowed to continue and over 70 per cent of MATs have fewer than four schools, so the cohesion of the system will, to a great extent, depend not only on the strength of co-operation within MATs, but how well separate MATs work together. The co-ordinating power of the RSCs will be important, but more important still will be the wider moral purpose of headteachers and governing boards to work for the common good.

The specialist carrot

The 15 city technology colleges (CTCs) established by the Conservative government in the 1990s were, as we have seen above, the building blocks for Tony Blair and Andrew Adonis to establish sponsored academies. Some of them, such as John Cabot in Bristol, have become successful groups of schools, with a strong social mission in disadvantaged areas. They were also the forerunners of specialist schools, which enabled secondary schools to take on a specialism, such as technology, science, languages or sport, and receive an initial grant of £100,000 (later reduced to £50,000) and additional revenue funding of £129 per pupil per year.

The Specialist Schools Trust, later the Specialist Schools and Academies Trust (SSAT), led by Sir Cyril Taylor, was as favoured by Blair and Adonis as it had been by their Conservative predecessors. The specialist programme expanded gradually from 35 schools, when applications were only accepted from grant-maintained or voluntary aided schools, and a limited number of specialist schools was allowed in each area, to nearly 3000 schools (90 per cent of secondary schools) by the time the incoming Conservative government ended specialist school funding in 2010. These schools could choose to select up to 10 per cent of their intake on ability in some of the ten permitted specialisms, although only a small proportion did so.

Introduced, and subsequently supported by both government parties, as part of a national agenda for greater choice and diversity, the SSAT became a school improvement movement of which schools were pleased to be part. They were provided with high quality performance data by Professor David Jesson of York University, although Cyril Taylor and the chief executive of the SSAT, Elizabeth Reid, did not always use the data to compare like with like when they claimed that specialist schools performed better than non-specialist schools.

ASCL and SSAT worked closely together on several initiatives, including the ground-breaking work, led by Professor David Hargreaves, on personalising education, the results of which were taken up in many secondary schools. I joined the Board of SSAT, a large gathering whose meetings were conducted bizarrely by Cyril Taylor as a succession of bilateral discussions between him and Board members, not necessarily on the agenda item that the rest of us thought we were on. The Board was eventually reorganised and Cyril Taylor was voted out as chairman. The SSAT prioritised its expansion through winning external contracts and lost its soul as a membership organisation. Losing contracts from 2010 onwards and continuing in its expensive Millbank premises led to it becoming bankrupt, but the successor SSAT, ably led by Sue Williamson, has maintained a loyal following as an effective school improvement organisation.

There was considerable opposition to specialist schools, but there was more to them than simply a way to increased funding. In the best days of the SSAT, when it was broadly based and most secondary schools were in membership, it formed a useful network firmly rooted in school self-improvement. Its Raising Achievement, Transforming Learning project (RATL), led by David Crossley, was one of the forerunners of school-to-school support, bringing together successful specialist schools with those in difficulty. The sports specialism, inspirationally led by Sue Campbell at the Youth Sports Trust, was a model of school partnership working, with all secondary sports colleges employing a specialist to work with local primary schools.

Geoff Barton, head of King Edward VI School, Bury St Edmunds, which had a specialism in sport, but which also gives priority to the arts and other enriching areas of school life, writes:

'Our school was energised by specialist status back in 2003. It not only got us evaluating our strengths and weaknesses. It got us thinking about how we could add distinctiveness to education locally by enhancing the specialist provision of neighbouring schools. It encouraged collaboration – we talked to local schools, visited other sports colleges, felt we were part of a national mission whereby, working together, we would contribute to the improvement of England's schools.'

There was thus a variety of approaches to specialist school status from head teachers. As an initiative, it was successful for most of its life because it not only provided secondary schools with a useful additional funding stream, but it gave them better and more rapid data than was provided by the government or most local authorities and this data could be used to benchmark the school's performance against similar schools elsewhere. It provided excellent training, good conferences and a strong network. As Geoff Barton found, it helped schools to put their values into action.

Leading a comprehensive school

Like all primary schools, local community comprehensive secondary schools serve their local communities and admit all the local children. It is therefore hard to fathom why these noble aims have remained solidly in place for the primary age group, while secondary comprehensive schools have been subject to the winds of policy change, reaching gale force at times.

I was proud to be head of a comprehensive school serving a defined area in and around the city of Durham. The school was, and remains, popular with local people and few children from outside the area obtain places. The local authority runs the admissions and the school teaches the children who are allocated a place. The full range of children attends the school – from the children of university lecturers and cathedral staff to the children of unemployed people living in villages that used to have a coal mine and struggled for long afterwards. Academic excellence has always been a top priority of the school, but its aims are much broader than this, offering opportunities to children from all abilities and backgrounds. The school's website home page summarises this:

'A commitment to social justice characterises this local authority comprehensive school. We work so that background is irrelevant to achievement and that aspiration is not limited by circumstance of birth. We want Johnstonians to be reflective, inquiring, tolerant, positive and respectful of the needs of others. We give opportunities for leadership and active citizenship.... We want to be central to the life of Durham City and an educational force in the life of the communities we serve.'

Coincidentally, while writing this chapter, I received an email from Abigail Moss, a former student at Durham Johnston when I was head there, and now director of programmes and partnerships at the Book Trust. She said: 'My Durham Johnston year group celebrated our 50th birthdays together in Durham recently. It was a fantastic party and demonstrated what a brilliant comprehensive education can achieve.' This was, and is, a school of aspiration and opportunity, as every school should be. Thus, while government ministers of both main parties talked of increasing choice and diversity between schools, we sought to offer diversity within our school, so that we catered for the needs of the full range of learners.

Building trust

When Tony Blair introduced the concept of trust schools in the mid-2000s, his parliamentary Labour colleagues were not impressed, seeing this new breed of schools as yet another tactic on the part of the prime minister to prise state schools away from local authorities. Indeed, Tony Blair's rhetoric about trust schools strongly gave this impression.

Although, as general secretary of ASCL, I had regular meetings with the education adviser in 10 Downing Street, I had only one one-to-one meeting with Tony Blair himself, when he sought my support for trust schools. I said to him that, if trust schools were a device to separate schools from each other, I could not support them but, if they were a means by which schools could work together, they would have ASCL's support. Then he quickly moved the subject on to A levels and how I thought they were doing!

A trust school is a maintained school supported by a charitable trust, with the trust managing the assets of the school, employing the staff and setting the admission arrangements.

I could hardly have imagined then the impact that the trust schools legislation would have in creating a vehicle for schools to cement their partnership working. From these small beginnings have grown MATs, of which a majority of schools will be part by 2020. We will look at the way in which trust schools are promoting inter-school partnerships in further detail in chapter 9.

Selection by ability

There remain 164 selective grammar schools across over 30 local authority areas in England. Of these areas, 15 have fully selective systems and it is difficult to attend any meeting of secondary school leaders without the elephant in the room, selection, trampling all over the discussion.

I have never been a supporter of selective education, believing that the best education for young people and the right way to develop a tolerant multi-cultural society is for young people to be in a school with others from different backgrounds and with different abilities. I enjoyed leading a school comprising young people from all walks of life.

I met a former Durham Johnston Comprehensive School student in Sainsbury's a few years after he had left the school. Now that he was in the army and recently graduated from Sandhurst, I asked him how he had found the predominantly independent school culture at Sandhurst. He replied that he had got on well with everyone and he thought that, because of the range of people at school, he had related much better to the regular soldiers than independent-educated officers-in-training. An important part of a comprehensive school education is developing social skills that enable young people to build good relationships and learn to treat the most junior employee of any organisation with the same degree of respect they accord to the boss.

The days when grammar schools were the route out of poverty for intelligent young people from lower socio-economic groups have long passed, with grammar schools now admitting only 3 per cent of disadvantaged students against a national average of 17.5 per cent. Those who fail to get into grammar schools are less likely to do well at GCSE than similar students in comprehensive areas.[18]

There are some excellent grammar schools, but their quality should not be considered in isolation from the secondary modern schools for those who fail

---

18   Financial Times, 28 January 2013

the 11-plus. Those calling for an increase in the number of grammar schools, such as Prime Minister Theresa May or Graham Brady, the Conservative MP for Altrincham, invariably fail to mention secondary moderns in their advocacy of more selection. The damage done by selection at 11 is long-lasting for those labelled as failures.

The move by Theresa May, in a green paper in September 2016,[19] to increase selective education will reduce the social mobility that the prime minister claims that she wants to increase. It will throw the school system into turmoil in some areas and make the job of leading non-selective schools harder. The claim by the prime minister that a new generation of grammar schools would be 'inclusive' attempts to defy the fact that selection is intrinsically exclusive.

Other types of school

Leadership of free schools, studio schools and university technical colleges was the subject of a report which I co-authored for the National College in 2014. Unless they were part of a larger chain of schools, the leaders of some of the first cohort of these schools had a torrid time against the near-impossible DfE timescale between approval and opening. They often struggled to appoint staff, recruit pupils, plan the use of a building, buy equipment, design the curriculum, write dozens of statutory policies or, in some cases, find a building in which the school could start work, which was not necessarily the same as the building in which the school would eventually reside.

Where this Herculean task was being undertaken by someone without previous headship experience, so that they were having to learn the rudiments of headship while preparing for the new school, expectation outstripped reality and not all survived in the job. My contact with the heads of some of these schools in the autumn of 2012, soon after the first cohort of free schools had opened, was generally through the head's mobile phone, since the school had no landline, BT having apparently been too busy with the London Olympics to be able to put in telephone lines for these new institutions. Ministers were happy though – they could say that 24 free schools had opened on time.

Free schools are, in legal terms, academies that receive a building grant. Thereafter, they are academies in all but name. Many of them were established in the teeth of opposition from existing local schools, but the future health of the school system in each locality will depend on school leaders working together, whatever the designation of their schools may be.

In the case of university technical colleges and studio schools, this will be

---

19   Schools that work for everyone, HMSO, 2016

particularly important, as the failure to work with other local schools places these new institutions, which recruit 14-year-old students from other secondary schools in the area, in danger of being too small to be viable and some have closed within a few years of opening. As part of a planned network of local schools, with their leaders working together – perhaps under shared leadership within a MAT – university technical schools, studio schools and free schools should all potentially have something distinctive to add to local provision.

***

It is almost impossible to conceive of a more complex system of school types than the secondary schools in England. With almost all of the 19 different types of school still in existence and the age of transfer varying from 8 to 14, the government's aims of diversity and choice have clearly been achieved, but this has come at an immense cost. In many parts of the country, incoherence is the only word to describe the situation in 2016. Parents are confused and the interests of the school system as a whole have been sacrificed to the focus on individual schools, through structure, funding mechanism and accountability, conflicting with the need for policy priority on schools working together, as we shall see in chapter 9.

The needs of learners cannot be met by a one-size-fits-all education, but it was a calumny to imply, as politicians did repeatedly in the 1990s and 2000s, that comprehensive schools all offered the same type of education. The pejorative 'bog-standard comprehensive', damagingly articulated in 2001 by Alastair Campbell when he was Tony Blair's communications chief, made my blood boil at the time and still riles me years later.

Leading a primary, special or secondary school of any type has never been formulaic and one only has to visit two schools to recognise that history, intake, values, staffing, buildings and many other factors all play a part in creating the uniqueness of a school. The challenge of leadership is to take all those things and mould them into an institution with the highest standards in every area of school life, and which gives all young people the opportunity to raise their aspirations and make the most of their talents.

The notion that governments need to create many different types of school in order to offer a diversity of types of education is based in political rhetoric rather than supported by evidence.

In England, diversity always seems to turn into hierarchy, a tendency in the school system that has been accentuated by the operation of accountability measures. The pursuit of 'diversity between schools' has made the task of leading some schools extremely difficult and the support systems have not been in place to level the playing field for schools adversely affected by policies promoting diversity.

The rich history of schooling in England suggests that, under any system, schools develop their own ethos and characteristics and this is one of the greatest attractions of leading schools in this country. If, however, there is a high degree of similarity in what schools teach, this is because governments have contradicted their own rhetoric of 'diversity and choice' through ever-increasing centralisation of policy.

'Diversity and choice' should be replaced as a political mantra by 'high standards through autonomy in a climate of collaboration', thus focusing on standards instead of structures and emphasising that autonomy for schools only works well for the system as a whole when it is within an over-arching collaborative structure. The government needs to put in place policies that encourage this and school leaders must respond to the challenge of working in this way, as many have already done.

In an ideal world, plans could be set out for a more coherent, understandable system of secondary schools to complement the community primary schools serving the younger age group, but political reality suggests that this would be setting unattainable goals for the foreseeable future.

While resisting an increase in selection at the age of 11, which would be damaging to the life chances of many young people, it seems sensible to recognise that the most important aspect for school leaders is how they can work within the current pattern of schools to improve the system as a whole, as well as the individual school that they lead. Multi-academy trusts provide the template for schools to work in partnership, both for primary schools and within the incoherent system of secondary schools described in this chapter. The ways in which they can best do this are discussed in chapter 9.

Chapter 3

Leading the curriculum

*Education is the most powerful weapon which you
can use to change the world.*
Nelson Mandela

My definition of the school curriculum is everything that happens to a learner in school. It is not only the subject matter of lessons; it is the whole school experience, including what happens in lunchtime and breaks, extra-curricular activities and school visits.

In the independent sector and in a minority of maintained schools, extra-curricular activities are called co-curricular, thus emphasising the way in which this part of school life is regarded as part of the curriculum. Indeed, Tony Little, the former headmaster of Eton, goes further, stating that there are two 'fundamental truths' to school life – that young people learn as much outside the classroom as in it; and that young people learn more from each other than they do from adults.[1]

Taking this expansive view of what constitutes the curriculum is a liberating approach, enabling school leaders to plan a broad and balanced curriculum that prepares young people for work, life and further study.

---

1   Tony Little, An intelligent person's guide to education, Bloomsbury, 2015

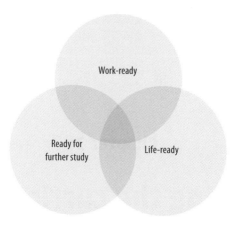

Figure 1

The relationship between the school curriculum and the national curriculum is an important one since the national curriculum is not, and was never intended to be, the whole of what young people learn in school.

The national curriculum was introduced for the very good reason that there was too much variation in what pupils learned in different schools, making it very difficult for the many children who have to move from one school to another during primary or secondary school. The national curriculum also brought a welcome degree of coherence and progression to the 5-16 curriculum. No longer would pupils study the Romans three times and the Tudors not at all.

Unfortunately, the first English national curriculum, which was planned during the second half of the 1980s, was written by ten separate subject groups, with little overall co-ordination, and the sum of the parts added up to at least 120 per cent of the available time in a school year. While secondary school teachers worked their way through the folder for their subject, primary school teachers had the impossible task of absorbing and 'delivering' the contents of all ten folders.

As well as the problem of volume, the top-down nature of the curriculum, encapsulated in the word 'delivery', changed the face of teaching in England. In my vocabulary, 'delivery' is for postmen, milkmen and midwives. Education – literally, drawing out – is an interactive process in which both teacher and learner engage constructively and creatively.

Gradually, the top-down curriculum, set out in mind-numbing detail, took control of teachers' thoughts and actions so that, when the government began to slim down the curriculum, many teachers became frightened to teach material beyond the prescribed canon. The problem had been compounded by

Ofsted's compliance approach to the inspection of classroom teaching and the perceived need to produce a ton of paperwork to prove what had been taught. Many teachers have become dependent on instructions from above, with the consequence that their lessons are often unadventurous and formulaic. As Dr Bernard Trafford, head of the independent Royal Grammar School, Newcastle-upon-Tyne, eloquently put it in 2010:[2]

'Prescription has made us dependent. This is Stockholm syndrome, where hostages develop an emotional bond with their captors. The dependency culture in schools is insidious: it grows without us realising it, and becomes hard to break out of. That is where we are now. We have been demanding freedoms, insisting that big government back off, but when the tide turns and leaves the empty ground in front of us, we feel lost. It is scary out there, for sure. But how exciting that scariness can be, if schools and teachers free themselves to apply their creativity and inspiration as they judge best. We need to rediscover the confidence to devise our own curricula ...'

In the words of one headteacher to the National Education Trust, *'the only thing teachers hate more than being told what to do is not being told what to do.'*

As a head of the maths department at Framwellgate Moor Comprehensive School in Durham in the 1970s, I was in the fortunate position of being able to choose to do Mode 3 Certificate Secondary Education (CSE) with students who were unlikely to pass O level. Whilst I hated the sheep and goats nature of O level and CSE and later welcomed the introduction of GCSE in 1986, CSE mode 3 was a liberating mode of assessment that enabled me to plan a syllabus matching the needs of the young people in the school, set examinations that tested knowledge of the whole maths syllabus, mark them and award grades. The assessment aspects of this will be discussed in the next chapter, but I particularly welcomed the curriculum freedom.

As a teacher of maths, one of my prime aims was to try to ensure that my students enjoyed the subject. Too many parents tell their children that maths is hard and they could not do it when they were at school, with the implication that one can fail at maths and still be a success in life. I recall an annual conference of the Mathematical Association in Liverpool in 1975 when we were welcomed to the city by the Lord Mayor, the gist of whose speech was 'I was no good at maths at school and I am the Lord Mayor of Liverpool. You are all good at maths and you hold much less important positions.' In pursuing the aim of enjoyment, I used mathematical games to reinforce the learning of some concepts and I had a stock of maths puzzles and investigations in my desk drawer to give to students at appropriate times.

---

2   Times Educational Supplement, 29 October 2010

Enjoyment should always be a part of learning and no curriculum is complete without enjoyment as a core ingredient.

Relevance is important too and, while most of the school curriculum covers knowledge that is of universal significance, there should be space for a local element in the curriculum. Students in Durham and Devon should learn not only the knowledge set out in a national curriculum, but what is of particular relevance and interest in their locality.

The Royal Society of Arts (RSA) put the case for an area-based curriculum which, it argued, would help to engage young people and would draw on local resources to support their learning. Its report in 2010[3] recommended a set of principles to guide and underpin the design and operation of such a curriculum.

Social action is one element of an area-based curriculum, which has its place both within personal and social education in the classroom and in practical terms in the local community. Both theoretical and practical aspects should be part of the education of every young person.

Curriculum innovation is essential for the life of a school. Without it, teachers can too easily become narrow in their approach, limiting their focus to the confines of an externally imposed syllabus. Teachers are unlikely to be innovative in a school that takes a risk-averse approach; the example must come from the leaders of the school being innovative themselves and, through their actions and decisions, giving teachers implicit permission to innovate.

Every school should plan a curriculum that is thorough, covers both knowledge and skills, embraces international, national and local contexts, and is relevant to the present and, so far as can be discerned, future needs of the students. It should be fit for the young people of the 21st century and should be deeper and broader than the mid-20th century curriculum that education ministers since 2010 have recalled from their own selective schooling of 30 to 40 years ago and which they persist in imposing on all schools.

External constraints mean that few schools go back to first principles and ask the question 'What curriculum is appropriate for a young person in the 21st century?' One school that has done this is the all-through School 21 in Newham, led by Tony Blair's former speech writer, Peter Hyman, who left 10 Downing Street to become a teaching assistant and has become a thoughtful and inspirational school leader. His opening message on the school's website sets out the innovative aims of the school:

---

3   The RSA area based curriculum: Engaging the local, Royal Society of Arts, December 2010 www.thersa.org/globalassets/pdfs/reports/rsa_abc_concept_note. pdf. This was followed by Louise Thomas, Re-thinking the importance of teaching: curriculum and collaboration in an era of localism, RSA, 2012

'At School 21 we want to create an extraordinary place of creativity and learning. We are driven by our twin values of integrity and humanity and a desire to make our school full of joy and wonder. When I'm asked what the aim of School 21 is, I say that we want our children to create beautiful work and to make a difference to the world. If they achieve both these things, then future success will follow. We are a group of teachers who believe that learning is magical and that there is no barrier to what a child can achieve. If each child learns what it takes to create beautiful work, work of true quality, work that has required many drafts until it is as good as it can possibly be, then children will have learnt a lifelong lesson. And if every child learns how to make a difference to the world, how to get the most out of others, make life that bit better, then they will be equipped to do something special with their life.

My job is to make this possible. To recruit the finest teachers and educators, mentors and project designers, coaches and subject specialists and to ensure they are trained in the skills of 21st century teaching. Then to give them the freedom to plan incredible learning.'

School 21 prioritises the development of oracy as much as literacy and emphasises six main characteristics: eloquence, spark, professionalism, grit, craftsmanship and expertise, giving young people the opportunity to put these into practice, aiming for beautiful work through the drafting and re-drafting of their efforts.

Shireland Collegiate Academy has long been at the forefront of using IT for learning. With its e-books and flipped learning[4], it has taken this to a new level. Shireland serves the highly disadvantaged area of Smethwick in the West Midlands and its approach is central to its delivery of the creative and rigorous curriculum that it believes best suits the needs of its learners. E-books have facilitated the flipped learning and given students much greater and faster access to a wide range of learning materials. They also enable the school to tailor the curriculum more closely to the needs of every learner, encouraging reading among all students, including reluctant readers, and enabling classroom time to be used more efficiently. Kirsty Tonks, director of e-learning at Shireland, says that this approach has been driven by the students themselves: *'They've said that finally the academy has caught up with them in terms of accessing things through electronic means.'* [5]

---

4   Flipped learning, sometimes referred to as the flipped classroom, is a form of learning in which instruction that normally takes place in the classroom is done at home, generally online, with classroom learning changing to include what would have been done as homework.

5   SecEd, 22 May 2014

Taking the definition of the curriculum as the whole school experience and discussing with staff, parents and the local community about what curriculum the young people need can create a dynamic basis for learning. This can be built upon in innovative ways by an outward-looking school staff. There is no shortage of material available online, with leading sites such as the quality assured TES resources or the superb material placed online by individuals such as Ross Morrison McGill at Teacher Toolkit.[6]

The government's role in the school curriculum

The elected government has a role to play in defining the school curriculum, but this should be at a framework level, leaving room for innovation and localism. Alas, the government in England has found it politically useful to define the detail of the curriculum in ways that, when associated with national assessment and accountability, have often ended in tears.

We have had ministers making policy on their pet subjects – Kenneth Baker on history, Michael Gove on English, Nick Gibb on phonics, almost everyone on Shakespeare and mathematics. In early 2010, Nick Gibb told me and everyone else he met that, if they wanted to know what a Conservative government would do in education after the general election later that year, they should read E. D. Hirsch's 1987 book[7], with its emphasis on a knowledge-based curriculum. He and Michael Gove subsequently proved to be faithful disciples of Hirsch.

Curriculum and qualifications for 14 to 19 year olds

The opportunity to bring the Key Stage 4 curriculum into harmony with post-16 in a unified, coherent 14-19 qualifications structure was lost when Tony Blair vetoed the recommendations of the Tomlinson report[8] in 2004, leaving an unreformed system that lacks continuity at age 16.

As secretary of state, Ed Balls tried to bring some coherence into the 14-19 phase with the introduction of a diploma structure, but this was far from universally popular and Michael Gove was decisive in abolishing it in 2010, with considerable support for his decision. The vast majority of secondary schools had put a huge amount of money and planning into the implementation of the diploma and many had started down the road. Some, however, were not

---

6   www.tes.com/teaching-resources/ has millions of well-signposted resources.
     www.teachertoolkit.me/ and the associated twitter feed from
     @TeacherToolkit provide an excellent range of teaching strategies and ideas.
7   E.D. Hirsch, Cultural literacy: what every American needs to know, 1987.
8   14-19 Curriculum and Qualifications Reform: Final Report of the Working
     Group on 14-19 reform, Department for Education and Skills, 2004.

convinced by the diploma and held their fire. Andy Buck recalls the tough decision not to engage with the diploma: *'We just weren't convinced it was going to work in practice. This was most definitely a risky strategy, as government had set a date when all schools needed to provide their pupils with access to the range of Diploma qualifications. But it was a calculated risk and one based upon doing what we thought was right for our pupils.'* [9]

The extended project qualification (EPQ) was to be part of Mike Tomlinson's recommended 14-19 qualification and became part of the diploma. It has many merits, including its flexibility, freedom of topic choice, and the inclusion of research skills. As a free-standing AS, equivalent to half an A level, it represents an excellent way in which a post-16 student's curriculum can be given greater breadth and depth.

The EBacc has taken the place of the diploma in placing big demands for change across secondary schools. Government ministers have decided that all – or nearly all – students will benefit at key stage 4 from a mainly traditional curriculum diet of English, maths, science, humanities and modern languages, with PE and RE in addition, and have used the accountability system to drive curriculum change for 14 to 16 year olds. When this was first introduced, the accountability measure was put in place with less than two years' notice, so that 14 year olds had already embarked on their GCSE courses. It was quite shocking to see the rate at which some secondary schools reacted to the new measure, encouraging some students to change their subject choices, or take an additional subject in twilight time, in order to jump through the EBacc hoop.

With the accountability measures inviting schools to pursue qualifications – sometimes of doubtful quality – for league table places, there was an open goal for Michael Gove to initiate reform of just about every aspect of the 14 to 19 phase. With the changes in GCSE syllabuses and examinations, new syllabuses for A level, AS uncoupled from A level, a new grading structure, the EBacc, and new accountability measures at both 16 and 18, secondary schools will be running to keep up with the implementation of so much that is different. Taken together, this amount of change places unreasonable expectations on teachers and, more importantly, will create a difficult time for the guinea pig students in this age range until the changes are embedded.

The EBacc appears to be having a particularly damaging effect on arts subjects at Key Stage 4. It reduces the number of options a learner can take at Key Stage 4 and school leaders fear that the greatest impact will be on take-up in the arts

---

9   Andy Buck, Leadership matters: how leaders at all levels can create great schools, John Catt Educational, 2016, p.38.

subjects. I am with Sir Ken Robinson in believing that: *'The arts are among the most eloquent expressions of human intelligence, imagination and creativity. They beat at the heart of human life and give form and meaning to our deepest feelings and our highest thoughts.'* [10]

The EBacc has reinforced a hierarchy of subjects in secondary schools, with English and maths at the top and the arts at the bottom. To some extent, this hierarchy has always been present in the curriculum planning of many schools, with the arts allocated a smaller amount of teaching time than the core subjects. As long as the EBacc survives, however, the arts will not feature on the curriculum of the vast majority of 14 and 15 year olds, and that is wrong for the young people and wrong for society.

In 2015, the Warwick Commission report on the arts[11] stated that, between 2003 and 2013 there was a 50 per cent drop in GCSE entries for design technology, 23 per cent for drama and 25 per cent for other craft-related subjects. In 2012-13, only 8 per cent of students combined arts and science at AS level. The number of arts teachers in schools fell by 11 per cent between 2010 and 2015 and in secondary schools where a subject has been withdrawn for 14- and 15-year olds, drama and performance has dropped by 23 per cent, art by 17 per cent and design technology by 14 per cent. GCSE entries in music dropped by 9 per cent between 2010 and 2016.

The report highlighted the importance of the arts not only in the life of the nation but in the economy, with the sector valued at £76.9 billion, or 5 per cent of the economy. The artist Bob and Roberta Smith said that C P Snow's 'two cultures' distinction of 50 years ago – in which society was split into science and the humanities – had been made *'irrelevant by the emergence of the power of digital technology'* and that *'we must totally overhaul the importance of art, design, dance, craft and drama, and teach them in a more contemporary and computer literate way to every child so that we do not deny our young people access to a £76.9bn economy'.*

The Warwick Commission noted that arts audiences are overwhelmingly middle class and white, with low participation from most ethnic minorities, lower social groups and people who struggle financially. This is a good reason why the role of schools is so important in the arts, and why arts education should be an entitlement for all children and young people. In the words of the arts broadcaster, Melvyn Bragg, *'investment in the creative arts is the key to the*

---

10   Times Educational Supplement, 23 January 2015
11   Warwick Commission, Enriching Britain: Culture, Creativity and Growth, 2015, www2.warwick.ac.uk/research/warwickcommission/futureculture/finalreport/

lives of so many people in this country, and to the richer life of the country itself.'

In 2016 Andrew Lloyd Webber gave £1.4 million to London schools to pay for musical instruments and lessons in the capital, a sum matched by the Charles Wolfson Charitable Trust. That is great for children in London but, in other cities and in rural areas where there is particularly poor access to the arts, the need is even greater and the responsibility falls squarely on schools.

I have never been into a really good school that does not emphasise the importance of the arts, with wonderful displays of art in the foyer, frequent music and drama performances and a strong place in the curriculum. These schools know that, while much of what is learned at school gets forgotten, the experiences that children have in the arts stay with them throughout their lives.

Many schools use some of their pupil premium funding on the arts, giving children from disadvantaged backgrounds access to music and the other arts, by hiring musical instruments, paying for individual and group tuition, paying for visits to galleries and other arts events. This is an important part of levelling the playing field for children who do not have these opportunities at home.

The government prioritises STEM subjects (science, technology, engineering, maths). It is time that STEM became STEAM.[12]

It is to be hoped that school leaders and governing bodies will say about the EBacc, as Robert Hill has encouraged them in a blog post, 'Up with this we will not put', and refuse to subjugate the needs of students to their school's position in flawed league tables.

All school leaders should be able to put their hands on their hearts and tell themselves truthfully that every 14 and 16 year old was guided on to the course that was right for their ambitions and abilities. This has been made more difficult by the EBacc, and by Alison Wolf's report on vocational qualifications and the government's enthusiastic adoption of its recommendations to limit the number and extent of courses well suited to the needs of some young people. It is true that some students did courses leading them to places where they could not fulfil their potential and it is right that these learners should study a more academically rigorous curriculum, but the EBacc is not right for everyone – or even for the 90 per cent the government says it wants to see following an EBacc curriculum.

---

12   The above paragraphs on the arts in schools first appeared in my regular weekly online blog for the Times Educational Supplement, 1 August 2016, www.tes.com/news/school-news/breaking-views/ebacc-means-arts-are-absent-curriculum-vast-majority-and-wrong. The acronym STEAM adds the arts to the four STEM curriculum areas.

The EBacc harks back to an era when male government ministers were in short trousers and learning their gerunds in Latin. It is not a baccalaureate and it is not right for many of the learners who will have to follow it. The Tomlinson curriculum and qualifications were planned with the needs of a wide range of young people in mind and the sooner the dust is blown off that report and a new version of it developed, the better it will be for the education system in England and for the young people to develop their many talents to the full.

Other baccalaureate-style qualifications are emerging that school leaders can consider. In addition to the well-established International Baccalaureate (IB), there are the Welsh Bac, AQA Bac, TechBac and ModBac. The Headteachers' Round Table has also developed a Bac model qualification. School leaders who are seeking a better curriculum for 14 and 15 year olds will do well to consider whether any of these suits the aims of their schools.

School visits and exchanges

For disadvantaged children, the wider curriculum, or co-curriculum, is particularly important, as these pupils will generally have had a much narrower range of experiences outside school than their better-off peers. This is examined in more detail in chapter 6, but, in the context of designing a school curriculum, this aspect of school life should be included in planning and should be especially taken into account when considering how curriculum design can contribute to an equitable school experience for all, whatever their background and family circumstances.

Visits are an important part of school life and foreign visits and exchanges add a huge amount to the experience of learners, even if they do these things with their parents in the holidays. For those whose parents cannot afford the luxury of a foreign holiday, it is particularly important that the school provides the opportunity. Going away with one's peers, with school staff in charge, is a wholly different experience from a holiday with parents. To this day, I remember my first visit abroad – at age 14 on a school exchange to Le Mans, but not, alas, at race time.

Durham Johnston School had exchange visits with schools in France, Germany, Russia, Estonia and New York State during my time there, but the most innovative was an annual exchange with Japanese high schools. This came about after the Nissan factory started the production of cars on an old airfield near Washington in 1986, about 15 miles from our school.

Realising that nothing about Japan appeared on any of the examination syllabuses followed in the school and so the students knew next to nothing about that country, and that Japanese young people probably knew nothing about the north-east of England, I decided to start an exchange. I telephoned the Japanese embassy the next day and they put me in touch with the Japan Foundation, the Daiwa Anglo-Japanese Foundation and the only school in England with an exchange programme, County Upper School, Bury St Edmunds and its teacher of Japanese, Mary-Grace Browning.

A day after my first telephone conversation with Mary-Grace, she phoned back to offer me a place on her school's forthcoming exchange visit to Japan, taking place just eight weeks later. The head of sixth form, Fred Wharton, joined the County Upper group and thus began an amazing experience for the 120 17 and 18 year olds who participated between the first visit in 1988 and the final exchange 11 years later.

The Durham Johnston groups visited three or four schools in different parts of Japan, travelling with a three-week rail pass on the shinkansen, the bullet train, between destinations. They attended lessons and stayed in the homes of the Japanese students with whom they were partnered and whom they hosted in Durham six months later. It was a life-changing experience for many of the young people, some of whom went on to teach English on the JET (Japan Exchange and Teaching) programme after they had graduated from university, some worked for Japanese companies and a few married Japanese partners.

The special ingredient in this exchange was the preparation. You cannot expect young people to board a plane, fly 8000 miles, travel around a strange country, stay in homes with people who speak little or no English, and gain maximum benefit from the experience. They needed to learn some language and – more important in my view – needed to learn about Japanese culture if they were to make the most of the experience. So those participating in the visit, including the Durham Johnston teacher who would lead the group (a different member of staff each year), had to attend weekly classes on Japanese language and culture for nine months beforehand. Alongside learning some Japanese language, they learnt about the Japanese family unit or '*ie*', the religions of Shinto and Buddhism, the concepts of '*uchi*' and '*soto*', '*tatemae*' and '*honne*' [13], bowing, presenting business cards, exchanging gifts, wearing slippers indoors and different slippers in the

---

13 Roughly translated, uchi and soto refer to inside and outside and the notion that inside things are clean and outside things are dirty. Tatemae and honne mark the distinction between public behaviour and one's real feelings. It was important that participants in the exchange understood these concepts in order to behave in the 'right' way in Japan and thus be accepted by their hosts. A small example is that blowing your nose in public in Japan is seen as rude, whereas sniffing is polite, the reverse of the custom in the UK. To guide us in these matters, we used Professor Joy Hendry's excellent book, Understanding Japanese society (Routledge, 1987)

toilet, tatami mats, having a bath, the history of the country and its education system. They visited a local Japanese restaurant to become familiar with the food, although not all the exchange participants could eat all the food presented to them in homes in Japan – fermented beansprouts for breakfast will be an abiding memory for many of the Durham Johnston students. I love Japanese food, but even I found the water snails a bit difficult to swallow. Spending three weeks in Japan was an immersive experience for those who took part; as I said to their parents at the meeting before they left, 'Your sons and daughters will be away for three weeks, but I must warn you they will return five years older'.

Curriculum entitlement

So this was much more than an exchange; the preparation lessons were part of the school curriculum for participants. This led to the school setting out an entitlement for all sixth formers, which included the entitlement to study a foreign language – French or German at A level, Russian or Spanish for a certificate, or Japanese for those attending the lessons described above.

A curriculum entitlement not only helps prospective students to understand what is on offer; it also acts as a discipline to the school itself to ensure that it offers what is in the prospectus. The curriculum entitlement at Durham Johnston is substantially the same in 2016 as it was when it was first introduced around 1990:

Every sixth form student at Durham Johnston has:

- An individual timetable
- A well-planned programme of academic work
- Built-in development of study skills in all courses
- Guidance and careers advice
- The opportunity for work experience
- Links with employers and higher education
- Opportunities for physical recreation and community service
- The opportunity to learn a new foreign language
- The opportunity to improve financial awareness
- The opportunity to demonstrate independent study by completing the extended project qualification (EPQ)
- An entitlement to continuing personal development.

The principle of a curriculum entitlement can be applied more widely to the school experience for learners of all ages.

Artists-in-residence

Prior to 1990 when LMS was introduced and we controlled our own budget, I tried to persuade the local authority art adviser[14] to put an artist-in-residence into Durham Johnston School for a short period, but he had a small budget and a lot of schools and he never managed to provide us with one. So, one of the first things I did in 1990 was to start a termly artist-in-residence scheme.

Once a year the heads of art, music, English and drama met to decide on the curriculum areas in which we would seek an artist-in-residence for the following three terms. Our model was to have a different type of artist in school for a week each term, working with teachers and classes to develop expertise in their specialist area. Northern Arts helped us to find the artists and the local branch of Sainsbury's, with which we had a school-business link, covered half the cost. At the start we paid the artists £400 for the week. Many different specialisms were represented among our artists-in-residence: a printmaker, a glass artist, a ceramicist, sculptors, painters, a composer, a drama producer, authors and poets.

The school's aim in arranging this programme of artists-in-residence was to highlight the importance of arts education and to broaden the understanding of the students in different areas of the arts. The programme certainly achieved this aim for the students who came into contact with the artists, but what was more important in terms of long-term effect was the way in which the artists extended the skills and experience of the school's arts staff, a legacy which improved the arts education of generations of Durham Johnston students who had not themselves had the privilege of working with the artist when they were in school.

The most memorable parts of this programme were the visits of poets (we could only afford a day of their time, but the effect was transformational) and we were fortunate to see in school Carol Ann Duffy, who was later to become the Poet Laureate, and Simon Armitage.

In 1996 one of our artists-in-residence was a local metal sculptor, Graeme Hopper, who had trained as a blacksmith, and who was commissioned by County Durham to work with Durham Johnston students on the production of a statue to commemorate the Battle of Neville's Cross, which had taken place 650 years earlier, partly on what are now the Durham Johnston playing fields. This formed the centrepiece of the school's Sculpture Park in its ambitious Festival of Culture in 2014.

---

14 All local authorities at that time had the full range of subject advisers, on whose services schools could call and who paid routine visits to the school. In my experience, few of them provided added value, but some were of great help in supporting the work of weaker subject areas.

Extending the curriculum

In the 1990s I became concerned at the narrowing of the curriculum being imposed on schools by the government. Believing that every young person should have an entitlement to a broad and balanced curriculum, I have always been a supporter of having a national curriculum, but this should be a framework of study areas, not the detailed prescription that was put in place in 1988.

The Durham Johnston sixth form curriculum entitlement offered a guarantee of breadth for that age group, but 11 to 16 year olds needed something more than what was then prescribed. So we instituted Activity Time on a Friday afternoon, when every member of staff and every student participated in an activity that was outside their normal learning and took place in mixed-age groups. Teachers passed on the enthusiasm for their hobby or special interest and students chose a different activity each term. Sport, the arts, technology, new languages, walking, chess, war-gaming, debating and much more were offered and the school experience for both staff and students was extended. Other schools have adopted different strategies to broaden the curriculum, including days or weeks when the normal timetable is suspended.

Developing skills as well as knowledge

Soon after I became head of Durham Johnston, I was watching our junior public speaking team compete against other local schools. Afterwards, I reflected with the teacher who had trained the team on the importance of presentation skills for young people and the fact that the only students who were being trained in public speaking were those who were best at it. Surely, we said, this should be something that all children should have the chance to develop.

Following that conversation, the English department took responsibility for developing presentation skills, so that every child in years 7 and 8 was taught how to speak in public and was given the opportunity to practise the skill in English lessons. The English staff chose the winning speeches from each class and we had an evening competition to decide the overall winner. But the main point of the exercise was to ensure that all 11 and 12 year olds learnt how to improve their public speaking and presentation skills.

The science and PE departments can quite easily absorb into their scheme of work for all young people the development of the skills of teamwork and working in groups. Other skills can be developed in different subject contexts in secondary schools, while primary schools can plan a progressive approach to skills development, with each class teacher building on the previous year's progress.

Schools can create their own list of skills that they consider important. A good starting point is Professor Guy Claxton's *Building learning power*,[15] in which he sets out very clearly ways in which schools can help students become strong learners.

Another way to start this planning is to read what the Confederation of British Industry (CBI) has to say about skills and attributes.[16] It believes that skills development has been neglected in national debates on the school curriculum. There is, the CBI argues, a set of behaviours and attitudes that determine personal effectiveness and should be fostered in schools. The CBI sees this as developing patterns of behaviour, using curricular and co-curricular activities to help bring out those qualities in young people such as resilience and integrity. The CBI recognises that the skills that businesses require in young people go beyond what it has hitherto called 'employability skills' that could be taught separately in the curriculum. It states: *'Behaviours can only be developed over time, through the entire path of a young person's life and their progress through the school system. Everything that happens in a school should embed the key behaviours and attitudes.'*

Another useful analysis of required skills is the University of Melbourne's project on the *Assessment and teaching of 21st century skills* (ATC21S)[17], which lists skills in four broad categories:

- Ways of thinking: creativity and innovation, critical thinking, problem-solving, decision-making and learning to learn
- Ways of working: communication and collaboration (teamwork)
- Tools for working: information and ICT literacy
- Ways of living in the world: citizenship (local and global), life and career, personal and social responsibility

An American project advocates the specific development of grit, tenacity and perseverance[18], which played well with the emphasis placed on character education by the former secretary of state, Nicky Morgan.

Staff, parents and local employers will help school leaders to devise the list that is right for their pupils and then the delivery of this element of the curriculum can be planned.

15   Guy Claxton, Building learning power, TLO, 2002

16   First steps: a new approach for our schools, Confederation of British Industry, 2012, www.cbi.org.uk/campaigns/education-campaign-ambition-for-all/first-steps-read-the-report-online/change-is-possible/

17   hwww.atc21s.org/

18   Nicole Shechtman et al, Promoting grit, tenacity and perseverance: critical factors for success in the 21st century, US Department of Education Office of Educational Technology, 2013

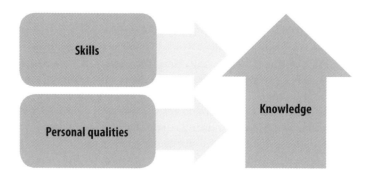

Figure 2 The warp and the weft of the curriculum

Skills cannot be taught in a vacuum; there has to be a context in which learners can develop skills. The planning of the curriculum therefore has to start with either skills or knowledge and use that as the basis. This can either be a skills-based curriculum, on to which the necessary knowledge is mapped; or it can be – and more usually is – a knowledge-based curriculum with skills worked in.

With a curriculum that specifies both, skills and knowledge are not taught separately; as knowledge is taught, skills and personal qualities are developed in a planned way. I like to think of this as the 'warp and the weft' of the curriculum, as illustrated in figure 2 above. In the example above, the English department at Durham Johnston did not stop knowledge-based teaching in order to teach presentation skills; the knowledge being learnt provided a context for the skill being developed.

In its *First Steps* report, the CBI pointed out that school systems in Singapore, Finland and other leading education jurisdictions follow this approach. It reminded us that in Finland, for example, the goals of education are explicitly linked to competitiveness, research and innovation. Singapore likewise has an explicit statement of the desired outcomes of education. The CBI report commented: *'All of these focus on defining a holistic vision of the young person they are trying to develop, encompassing knowledge, attitudes and behaviours – not just exam passes.'* On Singapore, the OECD has commented that: *'Students have the ability to think critically and solve real-life problems – skills that are valued in the society and at the workplace'* and the OECD also mentioned *'the strong link between education and economic development, as well as between policy and implementation in Singapore.'* [19]

---

19 PISA 2012 Results: Creative problem solving: students' skills in tackling real-life problems (Volume V), OECD, 2013

Whole Education

The development of knowledge, skills and personal qualities as part of a coherent curriculum is at the core of a fully rounded education. It was in 2010 that a group of people, meeting as part of the RSA-coordinated 21st century learning project, started Whole Education which I have chaired since its inception.[20] The essential message of Whole Education is that all young people – but especially those from disadvantaged backgrounds – should have an entitlement to a fully rounded education which, as we have seen above, is an important component of schooling in countries that have successful education systems.

In Sir Michael Barber's extended essay on education systems in Pacific region countries, *Oceans of innovation*[21], he concludes:

'What is clear, though, is that education – deeper, broader and more universal – has a significant part to play in enabling humanity to succeed in the next half century. We need to ensure that students everywhere leave school ready to continue to learn and adapt, ready to take responsibility for their own future learning and careers, ready to innovate with and for others, and to live in turbulent, diverse cities. We need perhaps the first truly global generation; a generation of individuals rooted in their own cultures but open to the world and confident of their ability to shape it.'

That surely describes a whole education in an international context.

The Whole Education Network is a national partnership of schools and organisations that believe all children and young people are entitled to an education that supports the development of wider skills, qualities and characteristics to enable them to thrive in life, learning and work, as well as in conventional academic achievement. Whole Education Network schools are developing different ways of achieving this common aim.

The Whole Education Network requires much more from its schools than mere academic achievement. The importance of well-being is emphasised, as are developing character and personal qualities and retaining students in lifelong learning. If a school's curriculum concentrates only on knowledge development, the school is missing much about what students know, can do, and care about.

In the English education system, society, schools, teachers and students end up valuing most what is measured. So the detail of what is measured and how it

---

20   www.wholeeducation.org

21   Michael Barber, Katelyn Donnelly and Saad Rizvi, Oceans of innovation: The Atlantic, the Pacific, global leadership and the future of education, Institute for Public Policy Research, 2012 www.ippr.org/publications/oceans-of-innovation-the-atlantic-the-pacific-global-leadership-and-the-future-of-education

is measured is important and this is discussed in chapters 4 and 5. The aims of most schools are committed to the broad purpose of education outlined above. Some learners in most schools benefit from a fully rounded education, but the system's current emphasis, in terms of both statutory assessment and accountability, is having the unintended consequence of many schools putting less emphasis on developing wider skills and attributes.

This has the greatest impact on the disadvantaged students who most need their schools to provide these educational experiences. It also has adverse implications for the country, since young people are not being fully prepared in a way that will enable them to maximise their contribution to our economy and society.

Whole Education's views were strongly supported in the CBI First Steps publication quoted above and the CBI Director-General at the time, John Cridland, who made a much more positive contribution to the education debate than any of his CBI predecessors, argued for greater emphasis on *'other factors that make a school system successful......that extends rigour beyond the merely academic'* and for *'a much clearer and broader statement of intended achievement for our school system'*.

The English system was traditionally, though perhaps less so in 2016, world-leading at testing and measuring conventional achievement and knowledge acquisition. It is much less good, and perhaps worse than it has ever been, in terms of valuing and measuring the wider purpose of education at a system, school and individual pupil level.

Whole Education argues for a 'both/and' not 'either/or' approach that recognises the importance of outcomes for young people in more conventional ways, but proposes that they are likely to be of more value and benefit if they are combined with a focus on wider skills and attributes.

This is supported by the findings of the Social Mobility and Child Poverty Commission in England, which stated that schools need to focus on developing these skills alongside improving academic attainment and highlights the importance of, in their words, *'Preparing students for all aspects of life, not just exams – supporting the development of character and other non-cognitive aspects of personality that underpin learning... It is not a question of either/or. Schools need to be doing both.'* [22]

Other reports in England[23] make the case for a focus on 'character and resilience'. They refer to, *'the growing body of research highlighting how character and resilience traits are directly related to being able to do well at school and in*

---

22   Social Mobility Commission, State of the nation 2014: Social mobility and child poverty in Great Britain, HMSO, 2014

23   For example, the Character and resilience manifesto published by the English all-party group on social mobility (Paterson et al., 2014)

the workplace,' concluding that, '*the so-called soft skills lead to hard results'.* They also stress the key role of policymakers and practitioners as these characteristics can be '*learnt and taught at all stages in life.'* [24]

Five steps to building a Whole Education curriculum

In planning a Whole Education curriculum – a fully rounded education for every learner –school leaders will need to take the following five steps:

- Recognise that education is the development of knowledge, skills and personal qualities
- Recognise that the statutory national curriculum is only a small part of the school curriculum
- Plan a curriculum that develops skills and personal qualities at the same time as knowledge, not as separate entities
- Enrich the curriculum by looking out for inspiration – locally, regionally, nationally, internationally
- Teach all elements of the curriculum as rigorously as the externally examined content

Leading teaching

Whatever the principles and detail of the curriculum in a school, the quality of the experience of the learner is dependent on the quality of the teaching. Leading teaching is the most important aspect of being a school leader and is discussed in chapter 8. For some teachers, considerable support is needed if the learners' experience is to be a good one; for others, it is a matter of standing back and giving learners the space to make the most of their proven skills. I was privileged to work with some truly inspirational teachers whose students went to university to read their subjects and who will have had a profound and unforgettable effect on those they taught.

The former Poet Laureate, Andrew Motion, has written[25] movingly about his English teacher, Peter Way, who inspired him with a love of books and of poetry. '*It's no exaggeration,'* wrote Motion, '*to say that in certain ways he gave me my life.'* This is the poem that Andrew Motion wrote the day after Peter Way's death on 30 March 2016:

---

24 Some of the above first appeared in the evidence of Whole Education in 2016 to the Select Committee on Education inquiry into the purpose of education. It is co-authored by David Crossley, Douglas Archibald and John Dunford.

25 Guardian, 9 April 2016, www.theguardian.com/books/2016/apr/09/my-hero-my-english-teacher-by-andrew-motion

My teacher, who reached down inside my head
and turned the first lights on. Who gave me Keats
to read, which turned on more. Who made me
read. Who made me write. Who made me argue
for the truth in things themselves. Who told me
manners maketh man. Who let me question
even the things he said himself were true.
Who gave my life to me, by which I mean
the things I chose and not inheritance.
Who showed a quiet voice can carry far.
Who took the gratitude I owed to him
and changed it into friendship. Who was kind.
My teacher, who died yesterday at peace –
his hardest lesson and the last of these.

***

In spite of the pressures on the curriculum from the government and its agencies, through accountability, curriculum prescription, national tests and examinations, it is still possible for outward-looking schools to develop a curriculum that best prepares their learners for life in the 21st century. It requires: a recognition that the school curriculum encompasses the whole school experience, not just what happens in lessons; an analytical approach to the needs of the students; an innovative climate in the school that encourages staff and students to be creative; enjoyment, relevance and a measure of localism; the planned development of skills and personal attributes alongside knowledge; and a relentless search for evidence of what works, locally, regionally, nationally and internationally.

It is ironic that, as the government has encouraged more and more schools to become academies and thus to be no longer subject to the national curriculum, secondary schools have become more constrained in their curriculum development by government prescription. Accountability is, as we shall see in chapter 5, a powerful weapon in the hands of government ministers.

But school leaders, acting together, can be powerful too, and it is profoundly to be hoped that they will collectively refuse to dance to the government's tune and determine anew that they will do whatever is right for the students in their care.

Just as the school curriculum should reflect the values of the institution, the school leaders themselves will need to adhere to the values of courage and collaboration in working together for a national curriculum framework that enables them to fulfil the needs of every young person.

Chapter 4

Leading assessment

When the cook tastes the soup, that's formative assessment. When the customer tastes the soup, that's summative assessment. Professor Paul Black

Assessment at the core of learning

In February 2016, Dame Alison Peacock, a primary head from Hertfordshire who is well respected both within the profession and in the Department for Education, suggested on Twitter that it would be a good idea to hold a profession-led conference on assessment. Alison wanted the conference to build confidence among teachers in the wake of the abolition of levels and start to wrest testing and examinations away from the government and its agency, Ofqual. The aim of the Learning First conference was to 'share strategies for high quality teaching that refuse to be dominated by ticking boxes, gridding or cramming', according to the conference website.

On 21 May 2016 several hundred teachers, school leaders and other educationists duly gathered at Sheffield Hallam University to share ideas and to gain a better understanding of the world of assessment after the government had ended the use of national curriculum levels to define pupil progress. Senior staff from Ofsted and Ofqual were present and Sean Harford, the director of inspection at Ofsted, earned a big round of applause when he said 'I'm here to listen'. Alison Peacock, whose success at Wroxham School is based on valuing every individual child and developing potential to the full, said in her introduction to the conference, 'If we forget to listen to the child, we miss a trick'.

Listening is an important aspect of assessment – listening to the learners, listening to parents and carers about their perspective on the progress of their children, listening to colleagues about their assessment experience and concerns, listening to other schools about excellent practice beyond one's own school, and listening to the professional assessment community at a national and international level.

Assessment is a two-way process, with teacher and student coming together to make each piece of work as significant as possible in the learning experience. This process lies at the heart of assessment for learning, with assessment and feedback the twin pillars of learner progress.

In their important book, *Inside the black box,* Professors Black and Wiliam defined the terms:

'We use the general term assessment to refer to all those activities undertaken by teachers – and by their students in assessing themselves – that provide information to be used as feedback to modify teaching and learning activities. Such assessment becomes formative assessment when the evidence is actually used to adapt the teaching to meet student needs.' [1]

Alison Peacock put this in the context of learning without limits:

'Recognition is growing that labelling is unjust. Building a positive state of mind, where colleagues refuse to see children as predictable or their future inevitable, offers a powerful alternative concept.' [2]

She gives an example of this at Nishkam High School in Birmingham, where the school community produced a set of principles, which included the statements[3]:

- *'All students can and will achieve*
- *Intelligence is not fixed; attainment is not pre-determined*
- *There should be no ceiling on achievement*
- *Students do not fail; they just have not succeeded yet*
- *Assessment as well as targets (and education) should enable, not limit*
- *Assessment is to support learning and the learner to make progress*
- *Marking and feedback are for students and should clearly describe what the students have achieved and what they need to do to improve'*

1   Paul Black and Dylan Wiliam, Inside the Black Box: Raising standards through classroom assessment, King's College, London, 1998
2   Alison Peacock, Assessment for learning without limits, Open University Press, 2016, p.4
3   Ibid, p.110

Speakers at the Learning First conference talked about getting the right balance between assessment for learning and assessment for accountability, and not allowing the latter to dominate the former. The day may well prove to be a milestone, marking the time when teachers began to reclaim assessment from the government and its agencies and turn it back into the support for learning that should be at its heart. This is a challenge that should be taken up by every school leader.

The purposes of assessment

Assessment serves multiple purposes and many of the problems experienced by schools in England have arisen from the use of the same assessment tools for multiple purposes, including: monitoring the progress of learners; feedback for teachers; test and examination results; grading learners for higher education and employment; school accountability through performance tables and a basis for Ofsted judgements; individual teacher and headteacher accountability through performance management; and monitoring the progress of national education standards.

It is a critical role for school leaders to ensure that assessment within school is fit for purpose and that the purpose of each assessment is clear.

It is equally important to plan assessment across the school, so learners have a consistent experience between subjects and from one year to another. Assessment for learning should support the aims of the school as a whole. When a school is part of a group or multi-academy trust, school leaders should aim for consistency across the partnership.

While it is part of the purpose of a school to prepare young people for external tests and examinations, assessment *of* learning should not dominate the learning process, but should complement assessment *for* learning. This is particularly the case when there are problems with the external tests, as there have been in the UK.

Examination and assessment problems

In 2003, I became increasingly concerned about the rising cost of external assessment for secondary schools and colleges. In many institutions, examination costs had become the second most expensive item on the budget, after staffing. The reasons for the rapid increase in examination costs at the time went well beyond the increasing fees being charged by awarding bodies for GCSE, AS and A level entries, although this was a factor. Many examinations were modular in structure and modular exams are more expensive than linear exams taken at the end of the course; students were, on average, taking more examinations;

vocational qualifications were growing in number and these tended to be more expensive than traditional academic subjects; and schools were spending more on examination administration and a lot more on invigilators. Putting all these factors together, the exams bill was going through the roof.

The problems with external examinations at GCSE and A level, in particular, are much deeper than their cost to school and college budgets. Although many of these problems surfaced during the Labour government's term of office from 1997 to 2010, ministers did not set up the major review of examinations and assessment that was required. Michael Gove and Nicky Morgan, as Conservative secretaries of state, carried out wholesale reform of the examination system without having first had a thorough review or piloting any of the changes, so the problems roll on.

The government has de-stabilised the system. GCSEs and A levels have a new structure and new content; AS level has changed from being the first part of A level to a standalone examination; the Diploma has been abandoned and the EBacc introduced; vocational qualifications have been changed; new accountability measures have been introduced; the grading system changed; coursework assessment largely abolished and terminal examinations increased. So the sheer volume of change in GCSE and A level examinations has become a problem in itself, making comparisons between years difficult; successful implementation in schools a major challenge; and rendering it impossible to evaluate any single change, so we are unlikely ever to know objectively how individual aspects of the new system are succeeding.

Ofqual itself has stated in a report in 2016[4] that *'performance on high stakes assessments is often adversely affected when that assessment undergoes reform, followed by improving performance over time as students and teachers gain familiarity with the new test.'* Ofqual calls this the 'sawtooth effect'.

When the government's own regulator is saying that the system has been destabilised in a way that means that examination performance does *'not necessarily reflect changes in a cohort's overall mastery of the subject'*, we know there are major system-level problems with the volume of change. The Ofqual report states that it takes *'roughly three years for students and teachers to become familiar with the nature and requirements of new assessments, meaning that we can have greater confidence that any improvements in performance after this time were due to meaningful gains in that subject area, rather than just test familiarity. ... These findings offer a novel contribution to our understanding*

---

4   Ofqual, An investigation into the 'Sawtooth Effect' in GCSE and AS / A level assessments, Ofqual, 2016

of how quickly, and by how much, students and teachers are able to respond to education assessment reforms.'

There are substantial problems too with primary school tests, not least because of the direct influence of government ministers on their content. The minister for schools, Nick Gibb, is a strong proponent of phonics testing, which includes an emphasis on non-words, such as dov and vead, and on the sort of grammar that he himself learned at school more than 30 years previously. The linguistics expert, Dr David Crystal, was highly critical of the tests.[5]

The grammar test has serious implications for the teaching of writing, as many teachers feel forced to use isolated grammar exercises instead of teaching a coherent and integrated writing curriculum with strong links to reading and the wider curriculum. The result is that children are less likely to write fluently, independently or at length, adapting form and style for a range of purposes and audiences. The interim assessment framework from the government is compounding this difficulty, since teachers can assess children's writing for example, whether a child has used a semi-colon to separate independent clauses twice in the last six weeks – without actually reading the children's work in full.

The complaint is often raised that teaching has become too much 'teaching to the test', but that is not the problem. Teaching to the test is fine, provided the tests are of high quality and sufficiently broad, and provided that the tests are not allowed to define the limits of the curriculum. The main issue with tests for 11 year olds has been that the tests are not a good reflection of the broad content of education that schools want to give children of that age and they have caused teachers to narrow their focus.

A bigger role for teacher assessment

Part of the problem that engaged my attention in 2003 lay, and continues to lie, in the lack of trust in teacher judgement and the total dependence on external assessment. If part of each grade could come from reliable teacher assessment, I reasoned, the size of the external examination system could be cut and a large amount of scarce school funding could be saved.

The key word in that sentence is, of course, 'reliable'. When A level and O level were founded in 1951, the intention was that the examinations should continue until teacher assessment could be relied upon and then the exams would end. 65 years later, the system is even more dependent on external examination grades and teacher assessments are probably less trusted than ever. Assessment is a Cinderella part of initial teacher education, with too little time devoted to it.

---

5   Times Educational Supplement, 4 June 2016

Some good work is being done around the country in professional development on assessment, but the depth of work is insufficient to base external grades on the judgements of those who have been on a short course.

In 2003 I wrote a policy paper for SHA, concluding that the only way to reduce the exams bill and enable the system to put trust in teachers' judgements was to build a network of chartered assessors in schools and colleges across the country – senior professionals accredited to carry out internal assessment to external standards and acting as guarantors of the assessment judgements of other teachers. Each school, or group of small schools, I suggested, would have one or more qualified assessment experts, who would guarantee the standard of assessment in his or her school(s). Internally assessed grades could then provide, say, half the assessment of the final grade in GCSE and other external examinations, external assessment providing the other half.

Practical exams would disappear under this system, with the grade for practical work in science, technology and arts subjects being assessed throughout the year – a much more valid indicator of a student's ability in practical work than a single practical test on a hot day in May, provided that the grade was moderated by a chartered assessor.

The chartered assessor model has a parallel in modern languages speaking examinations, whereby the orals are conducted by a member of the school languages department, but, if a school has no teachers sufficiently fluent in the language being examined, it can ask the awarding body to provide an external examiner to carry out the oral test.

Dr Ken Boston, the tough Australian brought in by the government in 2002 to steer the Qualifications and Curriculum Authority (QCA) out of its difficulties, saw merit in the proposal for a network of chartered assessors and quietly put a small amount of QCA funding into an internal group to establish the concept. He kept it under the radar in order not to frighten DfE ministers and officials who were avid proponents of the need for assessment to be external. The Chartered Institute of Educational Assessors (CIEA) was established, gaining its Royal Charter after a year.

I agreed to join the CIEA board in early 2011 and, on the way to my first meeting, was asked to take on the chairmanship. This was not part of my retirement plan, but I regarded the development of a network of chartered assessors as vital and I agreed to become chair. This coincided with Michael Gove abolishing what was by then the Qualifications and Curriculum Development Agency (QCDA) – note the downgrading from authority to agency that had already taken place. The CIEA, which had hitherto been entirely under the QCDA umbrella and had received generous grants from the QCDA, had to become an independent membership organisation, with no government funding, from April 2011.

A successful CIEA will have a key part to play in the system, accrediting both examiners who work for awarding bodies and senior teachers who work in schools and colleges. If it can establish an extensive network of chartered assessors, there is some chance that public confidence – and that of politicians and government officials – in the assessment judgements of teachers can be built to an extent where it will be seen as an improvement to the external assessment and qualifications system to include an element of in-school assessment.

No doubt concern will be expressed about the reliability of teacher judgements in a high-stakes accountability system, but there is a built-in safeguard to such a system in that, in every subject, there would be an external element and an in-school element to the grade and, where the two parts are very different, the detail of the assessment could be moderated. Reliability would take time to develop, but it would be an immensely worthwhile goal.

In 1962 the Joint Matriculation Board (JMB) introduced an English Language O level with 100 per cent internal assessment by teachers, which became available across the whole of England from 1977. It was a genuine attempt to enable assessment to follow learning rather than vice versa. This qualification, in which the whole range of learning was being assessed, placed demands on teachers to be trained and to attend moderation meetings. It was extremely popular with English teachers and had 200,000 entries by 1993, having translated into GCSE by that time.

The greatest proponent of teacher assessment I knew was Len Rowe, who was head of English at Durham Johnston for much of my time there. Len, who died in 2009, was one of the best teachers I ever had the privilege to work with. He was an inspiration to his pupils and to his colleagues. As a young man he had played rugby for Northampton and cricket for the county. As a teacher, he brought scholarship and wisdom to every lesson. He had, for many years, used 100 per cent coursework assessment at O level and GCSE, believing it enabled his pupils to demonstrate a much wider range of knowledge and skills than they could ever do in a time-limited terminal examination. '*Look at this portfolio of work,*' he would say to me. '*It contains evidence of achievement in every aspect of the course and the student's grade is much more valid than any written exam could produce.*'

Alas, government ministers did not see these portfolios and so did not share Len's evidence-based enthusiasm for grades based on coursework assessment. I recall a meeting with Eric Forth in 1993, during the brief period he was a schools' minister. I was advocating the merits of coursework assessment, but he knew better. 'We all know that teachers cheat,' he said dismissively and would not countenance it. When Margaret Thatcher's former chief policy adviser, Lord Brian Griffiths, was appointed as chairman of the School Curriculum and Assessment Authority, the death knell of coursework assessment was sounded and the 100 per cent coursework assessment in English was ended. Len Rowe did not wish to be part of the new examination-based system and, after writing a coruscating letter to Lord Griffiths, he retired at the age of 56 – a serious loss to the teaching profession of a highly principled man.

The state government in Queensland has long relied on 100 per cent teacher assessment to provide the final grade for students finishing school, although it is proposed to change in 2018 to a grade system that combines internal and external assessment. There is a strong emphasis too on teacher assessment in Scotland's Curriculum for Excellence.

The recommendations of the Tomlinson report[6] in 2004 included the following:

'At entry, foundation and intermediate levels, in place of existing GCSE-style examinations, teacher-led assessment should be the predominant mode of assessment, though an element of external testing should remain. The focus of external assessment and quality control should be on ensuring that teacher-led judgements are exercised reliably and fairly for all young people, through mechanisms such as:

- *inspection, monitoring and approval of institutions to carry out assessment;*
- *establishment of a network of Chartered Assessors to lead good assessment practice in each institution;*
- *teacher training and development;*
- *systems for monitoring, evaluation and professional development at institutional level; and*
- *national sampling of learners' work to ensure consistent application of standards between institutions and over time.*

At advanced level, assessment should remain a balance between external examinations and in-course assessment, drawing upon the new quality assurance arrangements to place greater weight on the professional judgement of teaching staff. Assessment of the core should combine in-course and external assessment methods.'

---

6   14-19 Curriculum and Qualifications Reform: Final Report of the Working Group on 14-19 Reform, Working Group on 14-19 Reform, October 2004 www. educationengland.org.uk/documents/pdfs/2004-tomlinson-report.pdf

Just as the original designers of O level and A level examinations recognised that teacher assessment had a strong role to play in a valid and reliable qualifications system, so Sir Mike Tomlinson and his working party, with a broad consensus of support almost everywhere except 10 Downing Street, planned to make high-quality in-course assessment a keystone of the system they recommended, reasoning that this would make the best possible link between formative assessment during the course and summative assessment at the end. A national network of chartered assessors was seen to be an important part of building the expertise for this.

The Assessment Reform Group (ARG), comprising established education researchers, thought the same, setting out how a summative assessment system including teachers' judgements, could be introduced[7]:

'Available research evidence leads to the conclusion that systems relying heavily on test results are found wanting in several respects, particularly in their ability to give a dependable, that is, both valid and reliable, account of pupils' learning. The negative consequences of summative assessment for learning and teaching can be minimised by appropriate use of teachers' judgements. A number of issues need to be addressed in implementing a system making use of teachers' assessment. Some key requirements are for: robust and permanent procedures for quality assurance and quality control of teachers' judgments; the provision of developmental criteria, which indicate a progression in learning related to particular goals; teachers to have access to well-designed tasks assessing skills and understanding, which can help them to make judgements across the full range of learning goals; and for pre-service and in-service professional development that extends teachers' understanding and skills of assessment for different purposes.'

The National Centre for Excellence in the Teaching of Mathematics (NCETM) has published an excellent set of tasks to support teacher assessment of mastery. There is scope for the development of these tasks (and associated tests) to support continuous formative assessment in Key Stage 2. With these in place, a rigorous system of teacher assessment could be introduced for this age group to complement, and reduce, external testing. The result would be a broader basis for judging a student's grade, resulting in a more valid and reliable result.

---

7   Assessment Reform Group, The role of teachers in the assessment of learning, 2004 www.nuffieldfoundation.org/sites/default/files/files/The-role-of-teachers-in-the-assessment-of-learning.pdf. The Assessment Reform Group was a voluntary group of researchers founded in 1989 by the British Educational Research Association (BERA) as the Policy Task Group on Assessment. In 1996, it adopted the name ARG and its meetings were funded by the Nuffield Foundation. The ARG was dissolved in 2010.

A system such as that advocated by the ARG is unlikely to be introduced in the short or medium term, but its desirability cannot be doubted. The stronger link between formative and summative assessment would be of benefit to the quality of education of the learners and the reliance placed on teacher judgements can only increase the professionalism of teachers and the regard in which they are held by the public. It is to be hoped that it will be on the agenda of the College of Teaching which, with Alison Peacock as its chief executive, will surely take a close interest in assessment as an area in which the professionalism of teachers can be recognised and developed.

This radical change is an important issue for school leaders because, if we are to move in this direction over the next ten years, schools need to start now to develop assessment knowledge and skills in teachers and to put the leadership of assessment at or near the top of the teaching and learning agenda.

Measuring what we value, not only valuing what we can easily measure

For schools that place a high priority on giving every learner a whole education – a fully rounded curriculum of the sort described in the previous chapter – it is important to measure progress in more than academic terms. Education should be more than the pursuit of good test results. The curriculum should drive assessment, not the other way round; the assessment tail should not be wagging the curriculum dog.

Since I started teaching in 1970, there have been just two periods when the curriculum was in the lead and assessment was designed to test the knowledge of that curriculum.

The first period was during the life of the CSE Mode 3, from 1965 to 1986. CSE was designed to cater for the 40 per cent of students below O level standard and was graded 1-5, with grade 1 equivalent to a pass at O level. It was overseen by 14 regional examination boards in England and Wales, separate from the General Certificate of Education (GCE) boards. Standards were maintained by regional moderators, who worked with groups of teachers to mark samples of coursework.

CSE Mode 1 examinations were externally marked on board-designed syllabuses, with coursework in addition. CSE Mode 2 had school-designed syllabuses examined by the board, but these were done by only a small minority of schools. In Mode 3 the teacher devised the syllabus, had it approved by the board, examined and marked it, with moderation by the board. Not surprisingly, Mode 3 was a popular option for innovative teachers, with as many as 10,000 different Mode 3 syllabuses in a single region. Teachers were able to influence all three Modes of CSE, with Mode 1 and 2 syllabuses designed by teacher-dominated committees.

Because CSE grade 1 was equivalent to a grade C pass at O level, teachers used it, as I did, to help students to pass the five O level threshold that was the stepping stone to further education and employment. Being in control of both the curriculum and assessment of the course was liberating, professionally rewarding and good for the students who gained qualifications from courses that were relevant to them.

The second period when the curriculum drove the assessment was the early years of the GCSE, from its introduction in 1986. GCSE syllabuses were planned by subject experts and the structure of the GCSE examinations reflected the curriculum in its balance of terminal examinations, coursework and practical tests. Different subjects had different assessment patterns, as appropriate.

Throughout the rest of the 45-year period during which I have been a first-hand witness of education policy, assessment has led and curriculum has followed. School leaders need to reclaim assessment as an essentially professional activity and match it to the curriculum needed by young people in the 21st century.

It is a comment on the governance of education in England, and on the extent to which the teaching profession has been prepared to accept instruction from the government, that there is such a strong dependence on narrow external terminal examinations and tests. The message has come down from the government: the skill of passing exams is valued above other educational knowledge and skills. This has placed a major disincentive on school leaders' desire to give young people a broader education, as many of the skills and attributes forming part of a fully rounded education, of the sort described in chapter 3, do not lend themselves to being assessed in this way.

Standardised tests can be used to measure areas such as pupil attitudes and employability skills. The work of Whole Education and two national assessment organisations[8], shows there is a range of approaches that can be used to support school self-assessment of the wider purpose of education at both a school and individual student level. This type of test is used by higher education to measure the extent to which applicants for undergraduate courses in health and other sectors would be likely to complete the course and be successful in the work place.

---

8   Cambridge Assessment and GL Education

A visit to Australia in 2016 convinced former schools' minister, Jim Knight, of the need to move from what he describes as an industrial model of grading and sorting students for higher education and employment to an examinations system that better reflects the needs of the 21st century labour market. In his blog post, he quotes Charles Leadbeater on the need for assessment to reflect a broader education and '*go beyond testing routine facts to test higher-order thinking, problem-solving and creativity*'. Good examinations, especially at A level, already do that, but there is too little of that in GCSEs.[9]

As Alison Peacock states in *Assessment for learning without limits*, good teaching is enhanced where learners are involved in the assessment process, with personal best being the target, not ranking or point-scoring:

'The richer and more open-ended the curriculum, the greater the opportunity for the teacher to assess understanding and misconceptions. ... Too often, learning can be dominated by tests and exams to the extent that students in many secondary classrooms are intolerant of any activity that does not have a direct link to what may be expected of them within a forthcoming test. The key is to create a learning environment where assessment is understood as a lifelong process of self-improvement and ambition, in the broadest sense.' [10]

Criterion referencing and comparable outcomes

Grading of students in A level and O level was traditionally norm-referenced, with a fixed proportion of candidates gaining each grade. It was Sir Keith Joseph, when he was secretary of state, in a speech at the North of England Education Conference in 1984, who recognised that this was unfair to students and meant that the country could never demonstrate system improvement unless it moved to a criterion-referenced marking system, in which levels of achievement to attain each grade are set before marking starts. This approach informed the grade descriptions in the national criteria for GCSE.

However, Ofqual, the government quango that oversees the examinations system, which has had five different names since 1988, has never managed to overcome the technical difficulties it has perceived to exist in a pure criterion-referenced model. Instead, in an attempt to reduce perceived grade inflation,

---

9   www.tes.com/news/school-news/breaking-views/why-we-must-move-away-industrial-model-schooling-just-grades-and; Charles Leadbeater, The Problem Solvers: The teachers, the students and the radically disruptive nuns who are leading a global learning movement, 2016 a4le.org.au/news/regional-news/the-problem-solvers

10   Peacock, op.cit., 2016, p.2.

GCSE and A level grade distributions are decided according to comparable outcomes, which are explained on the Ofqual website:[11]

'All exam boards must have awarding processes that meet Ofqual's rules, which are set out in a code of practice. The basic principle is that if the group of students (the cohort) taking a qualification in one year is of similar ability to the cohort in the previous year, then the overall results (outcomes) should be comparable. To do this, exam boards produce a reference matrix, based on the results of a previous cohort. This reference matrix, which compares Key Stage 2 attainment with the GCSE grades that this previous cohort achieved, is applied by each exam board to predict outcomes for the current cohort. For A levels, the starting position for predictions is the results achieved in GCSEs.'

Thus, subject awarding committees use the evidence of how well the cohort performed in Key Stage 2 tests five years earlier to predict the proportion of students likely to achieve each grade.

I accept that comparable outcomes help to maintain standards during the transition from one qualification to another, or from one syllabus to another (and there have been far too many of those changes), but I do not accept that this system needs to be applied all the time.

It raises the question of how the secondary school sector is ever to demonstrate improvement and it calls into question the data on closing the gap at age 16 and 18 between disadvantaged learners and others, which we shall examine in chapter 6. Under the controlling factor of comparable outcomes, one school's improvement must inevitably be matched by another's decline, even if the quality of teaching, learning and assessment is getting better in both places. With the limiting factor of comparable outcomes, there is no recognition that, like the world record for running the mile or the quality of aeroplanes, improvements over time are occurring in schools.

The representative bodies of school leaders and teachers should rise up and cry, 'Enough of comparable outcomes. Let us sit down and design a criterion-referenced system that is valid and that works.' Only then can the examinations system be fair to secondary school and college students and their teachers.

Bring back the APU!

The use of pupil-level data to monitor the progress of national education standards is highly unreliable, given that the same data is used for school accountability. The government sets the hoops for schools and teachers to jump

---

11   ofqual.blog.gov.uk/2015/08/05/gcse-marking-and-grading/

through and, not surprisingly, they jump through them. So test results improve and the government claims that the standard of education is improving.

In fact, the improving results largely show only that schools and pupils are doing better on the tests. It would be a much more reliable indicator of the health of the system to use sampling, as occurred during the period 1978 to 1988, when the Assessment of Performance Unit (APU) sampled the attainment of pupils at ages 11, 13 and 15 in English language, science, mathematics, foreign languages and design and technology.

From the school's point of view, this meant little additional work. For the 10 per cent sample, the school simply identified the children whose birthdays fell on the 5th, 15th and 25th of the month, put them in a room at a specified time and invigilated the test. The results, which were not identified by individual pupil or school, provided a reliable indicator of the progress of England Education plc. It was a bad day when the Conservative government abolished the APU. I have been a strong supporter of the 'Bring back the APU' movement, but nobody seems to have been listening.

The end of levels: a cause for mourning or celebration?

Levels were introduced with the national curriculum in 1988. The intention was to create an assessment system that measured pupils' progress against a national framework. The ending of levels in 2014 created both a problem and an opportunity for school leaders. On the one hand it highlighted the lack of confidence across much of the teaching profession and the lack of technical expertise in assessment theory and practice; on the other hand, it prompted a nationwide discussion about how assessment could be done better, with the prop of levels having been removed.

School leaders have taken this opportunity to review their school's assessment policy and practice and to put in place a post-levels system that measures progress effectively and enables teachers to share learning points with their pupils. The best of this practice needs to be disseminated more widely across the country and Alison Peacock has taken the lead on this with the courses based at Wroxham teaching school.[12] There is an opportunity for the CIEA to play a leading role in this dissemination.

While levels had their disadvantages, they provided a means of establishing consistency of standards across schools. With the end of levels, there is a tension between the recognition that assessment should follow learning and the maintenance of national standards. Thus school leaders experience difficulty

---

12   See also the case studies in Alison Peacock, op.cit., 2016

in ensuring that teachers of learners in the same year group have consistent expectations and that those are in line with national expectations.

This requires schools to be outward-looking in order to ensure formative and summative assessment are in line, with strong systems for moderation and an unambiguous approach to benchmarking of standards and expectations. If schools work in isolation, constantly reinventing the wheel, there is a risk that, after several years, they will suddenly find their assessments are way off the mark. These systems should be transparent and open and, as Mary Myatt says, 'high challenge and low threat', encouraging ambition but keeping in touch with reality.[13]

Professional development in assessment

A tiny proportion of postgraduate education certificate (PGCE) courses is devoted to the development of assessment knowledge and skills, so there is a high proportion of teachers who have entered the profession with undeveloped assessment skills and joined the staff of schools that do assessment much as they have always done it.

In-service training is therefore a vital component in the improvement of assessment in schools. Core policies should relate not just to teaching and learning, but to teaching, learning and assessment; in schools that are leading the way, the acronym TLA is in common use to signify the central place of assessment in their thinking.

Professional development is, as we shall see in chapter 7, about much more than going on courses, although this is an important element of improving practice in assessment at this stage in England. Assessment development should be central to the school's CPD policy, and there should be a senior professional who is a chartered assessor and with whom other staff have the opportunity to work.

School leaders can also beneficially encourage teachers to become examiners for awarding bodies, bringing them into direct contact with leading-edge assessment practice. In a joint article, the leaders of the main awarding bodies and of school leader associations in both the maintained and independent sectors stated that, *'Examining is CPD that trains you in assessment, enhances your understanding of the relationship between pedagogy and assessment, and develops your knowledge of what constitutes the required standard in a qualification.'* [14]

---

13   Mary Myatt, High challenge low threat: how the best leaders find the balance, John Catt Publishing, 2016
14   Times Educational Supplement, 27 November 2015

***

It is school leaders, however, who must ensure that their school's assessment principles are well-grounded in research evidence, that they have sufficient top-level assessment expertise on which to call, that their staff are well trained, and that the everyday assessment practice of teachers matches the school's aspirations for high quality teaching, learning and assessment.

The lead being taken by Alison Peacock and others in bringing assessment into a learning process based on trust and development – learning without limits – provides a challenge to all school leaders to re-evaluate their assessment processes and to judge the extent to which assessment is supporting learning and not just measuring whether learners have jumped through the next set of nationally-determined hoops.

If school leaders respond to these challenges, the profession will be in a better position to demonstrate that teacher assessment can be part of a valid, reliable system of tests and examinations, which will be a major improvement on the purely external judgements, based on time-limited performance in the hay fever season, and producing grades in which the public, as much as professionals, are steadily losing confidence.

For too long, teachers have been victims of a centralised and limiting national assessment policy. It is time that school leaders, individually, and collectively through ASCL and the NAHT, took command of the assessment agenda and, using the most up-to-date evidence available and encouraging good practice in every school, reclaimed from the government the professional territory that is rightly theirs.

Chapter 5

Leading accountability

*Plants don't flourish when we pull them up too often
to check how their roots are growing.*
Onora O'Neill[1]

Intelligent accountability in public services

Onora O'Neill's Reith Lectures in 2002, from which the above quotation is taken, introduced the notion of intelligent accountability and discussed trust and accountability across the public services in a way that made me recognise how unintelligent was the government's accountability regime for schools and what a low level of trust underpinned these accountability measures. As I was general secretary of the Secondary Heads Association (SHA) at the time, I wrote a paper which aimed to bring O'Neill's thoughts on intelligent accountability into the debate about school and teacher accountability.[2]

The paper was taken up by the schools minister, David Miliband, in a speech in January 2004 in which he set out a 'new relationship with schools', with intelligent accountability as one of the four pillars.[3] Six years later, at a general election hustings meeting hosted by the *Times Educational Supplement*, the education spokesmen of all three main political parties – Ed Balls, Michael

---

1   Onona O'Neill, A question of trust, the Reith Lectures 2002, Cambridge
     University Press, 2002 www.bbc.co.uk/radio4/reith2002/lecture3.shtml
2   Towards intelligent accountability for schools, Secondary Heads Association,
     2003. This paper is quoted extensively in a chapter on intelligent accountability
     in D. Hopkins, Every school a great school, McGraw Hill, 2007
3   schools.cbe.ab.ca/b352/pdfs/PersonalizedLearning_Building.pdf

Gove and David Laws – mentioned intelligent accountability within the first half hour. This should have made me very happy, but I realised that their policies were some way from their rhetoric.

The aims of this chapter are to discuss the system of accountability for schools and the way in which that impacts on school leadership, and to look at internal school accountability and how it can support the ethos of the school, the professionalism of teachers and the quality of education of the learners.

The starting point for my SHA paper in 2003 was an acceptance that schools are held to account and '*that proper safeguards are required for the spending of public money and the quality of public services. The public is entitled to reassurance that funds are being spent with propriety and that the service is efficient and effective.*'

I defined intelligent accountability for schools as:

'*a framework to ensure that schools work effectively and efficiently towards both the common good and the fullest development of their pupils. It uses a rich set of data that gives full expression to the strengths and weaknesses of the school in fulfilling the potential of pupils. It combines internal school processes with levels of external monitoring appropriate to the state of each individual school.*'

Thus, intelligent accountability is about *how* schools are held to account and *how much* accountability is needed. It is about both the quality and the quantity of the accountability measures. There are both internal and external elements.

Onora O'Neill's case was that the type and extent of accountability across the public services in the UK arise from a lack of trust in professionals. She described the way in which, since 1980, '*the quest for greater accountability has penetrated all our lives, like great draughts of Heineken, reaching parts that supposedly less developed forms of accountability did not reach. ... An unending stream of new legislation and regulation, memoranda and instructions, guidance and advice floods into public sector institutions. Central planning may have failed in the former Soviet Union but it is alive and well in Britain today. The new accountability culture aims at ever more perfect administrative control of institutional and professional life.*'

Onora O'Neill believed that lack of trust and the consequent ever-increasing government accountability diverted and damaged the work of the professions:

'*Teachers aim to teach their pupils; nurses to care for their patients; university lecturers to do research and to teach; police officers to deter and apprehend those whose activities harm the community; social workers to help those whose lives are for various reasons unmanageable or very difficult. Each profession has its proper aim, and this aim is not reducible to meeting set targets following prescribed procedures and requirements. If the new methods and requirements supported and didn't obstruct the real purposes of each of these professions and institutions, the accountability revolution might achieve its aims. Unfortunately I think it often obstructs the proper aims of professional practice. We are heading towards defensive medicine, defensive teaching and defensive policing.'*

O'Neill went on to explain how the culture of accountability was supposed to make institutions and professionals more accountable to the public by publishing inspection reports and league tables of results through which members of the public can complain about failures and take their broken leg or their child to a higher performing institution. But, she said, '*underlying this ostensible aim of accountability to the public the real requirements are for accountability to regulators, to departments of government, to funders, to legal standards. The new forms of accountability impose forms of central control.'* That is a feeling prevalent among school leaders and teachers.

Decentralisation of power in public services is almost always accompanied by a balancing increase in the power of the centre. Thus, in 1988, with school autonomy being increased through local management of schools and grant-maintained status, this was balanced by increases in accountability through a national curriculum, national testing and, shortly afterwards, a comprehensive system of individual school inspections.

The levers of government power over schools are primarily funding, accountability, and examinations and tests. As most schools become academies, no longer obliged to follow the national curriculum, this has ceased to be a strong lever. With schools in England having so much more autonomy than schools in most other countries, it is inevitable that central government will seek greater balancing power. Accountability is the other side of the coin of autonomy.

Perverse incentives

In discussing the perverse incentives created by performance measures, Onora O'Neill articulated what all teachers and school leaders have experienced for many years, that performance measures are too often chosen for ease of measurement and control rather than reflecting the complex process that is at the heart of educating the child. Pass rates in examinations and tests are only one aspect, albeit an important one, of education.

So perverse incentives are created by blunt measures and schools react accordingly, making policy choices that enable them to jump through the accountability hoops as successfully as possible – concentrating resources on students at the C/D grade borderline at GCSE, practising narrow tests for many months with 10 and 11 year olds, or choosing an easier GCSE or A level syllabus instead of the harder one that the teacher knows to be educationally superior.

External accountability drives policy in schools. Therein lies the power of central government to change practice at school level. For example, in 2012 schools were found to be entering students for GCSEs and International GCSEs with multiple awarding bodies, a flawed practice educationally, but understandable in the context of the high-stakes accountability system. The government announced that, in order to avoid students being entered for the same subject with many different awarding bodies, only the first entry would count in school performance tables.

School leaders were placed in the difficult position of deciding whether to enter learners for a 'practice' GCSE in the autumn, which would help them, but which carried the risk that lower grades would then count for the league tables. In the tension for school leaders between the position of the school in the GCSE league tables and the best interests of the learners, too often the school's reputation has won. Accountability systems should never be used in this way, incentivising school leaders to act against the interests of young people.

The announcement of an EBacc performance measure in 2011 was another example, with some schools adopting panic measures, as mentioned in chapter 3, in order to increase the proportion of their students gaining an EBacc – at least grade C in GCSE in each of English, mathematics, two sciences, a language and history or geography. In some schools, extra classes were put on at the end of the school day for students who were not studying the full EBacc range to do an extra subject. With the announcement made in October of their year 10, some students were asked to change their subject choice to comply with an EBacc curriculum; for example, to drop their second modern foreign language for history or geography.

With the EBacc defining a government priority list of subjects, schools are incentivised to react and give those subjects a stronger place in the school curriculum. A political value judgement has been made and educational consequences follow. Ministers have chosen not to prioritise the arts and, as we saw in chapter 3, arts education will suffer from its low place in the pecking order. If the government valued the arts more and gave it a different order of importance in the accountability system, league tables would look very different.

I spent many years trying to persuade government ministers that the threshold measure of five high grade GCSE passes was a bad accountability measure, since it incentivises schools to raise potential D grades to C, but does not encourage them to raise other grades. A much better performance measure, with the least perverse incentive, I said to ministers and DfE officials, would be the average GCSE (or equivalent) points score on students' best eight subjects. So I welcomed the change from the five GCSE threshold to the broader, non-threshold measure of Progress 8, even though it was more prescriptive than I would have liked.

Progress 8 is essentially a value-added measure based on grades in a defined group of subjects. Sam Freedman, who was a policy adviser to the secretary of state, Michael Gove, at the time, recalls how the problem with grades in GCSE English in 2012 revealed the extent of the distorting effects of the C/D borderline threshold as an accountability measure, with a very large number of candidates clustered around that borderline and therefore a small change in grade boundaries having a disproportionate impact.[4] In contrast, under Progress 8, the accountability driver will point schools towards policies that maximise the progress of all learners.

Under the pressure of the type of accountability described by Onora O'Neill from the government and its agencies, it is hardly surprising school leaders have come to regard accountability as something nasty done to them by Ofsted and the DfE. Even so, the high-stakes nature of external accountability means that the performance measures to which the school is subjected are passed down from the governing body and head to the teachers and other staff.

If the judgement on the quality of a school is the proportion of 11 year olds who gain level 4 in reading, writing and maths or the proportion of 16 year olds who gain at least five high grade GCSE passes, the system is encouraging headteachers to concentrate resources on the pupils just below those thresholds and hold teachers to account for the number of pupils they can haul over the threshold. Perverse incentives, as Onora O'Neill pointed out, are real incentives for heads and teachers in real schools.

Intelligent accountability within schools

After I had been a head teacher for five or so years, I looked again at the aims of the school and reflected that conventional performance measures of attainment and attendance, which were published, barely scratched the surface of what we were trying to do as a school. The breadth of our aims was in danger of being narrowed to a GCSE threshold statistic and the proportion of pupils absent over the year. As Rod Bristow, president of Pearson UK, wrote in 2015, Progress 8 is a better measure than five high grade GCSE passes, *'but it sits alongside other*

---

4   Times Educational Supplement, 26 February 2016

measures that are independent of exam results. This might sound complicated, but that's the whole point: a good education provides a range of outcomes, not just one.' [5] Accountability should promote, not inhibit, the pursuit of the aims of the school.

The need to avoid being driven solely by government measures caused me to do two things. First, my talk to staff on the first day of the autumn term each year mentioned the proportion of 16 year olds with five high grade passes, but focused much more on the average points score in their best eight subjects of the students in GCSE and other equivalent courses. It was this year-by-year line graph that I really wanted to see going upwards, to reflect the fact that the school's ambition was to raise the attainment of *all* pupils, not just those around the C/D grade borderline.

All threshold measures are bad performance indicators and create perverse incentives. As far as possible, we wanted to avoid that trap. The average points score graph sent a message to staff that every student's attainment mattered and that the school gave as much credit – even if the government did not – for getting a grade B student up to a grade A, or a grade F to an E, as it did for getting a grade D up to C.

The second thing that the aims of the school showed me was that we needed to measure our performance more broadly. To do it, we sought measures, or proxy measures, as performance indicators and I kept a record of these in a green ring binder, our IT systems being considerably less sophisticated in the 1980s than they are now in schools. Two examples of statistics from that ring binder will suffice to make the point.

One of the aims of the school was 'to maximise the opportunities for students'. So, as well as starting the school activity time mentioned in chapter 3, I kept a record of the number of students taking part in extra-curricular activities each year, the number going on visits, and the number taking part in school exchanges, as proxy measures for whether we were fulfilling this aim.

The second example related to staff development. We aimed to have a high quality staff who were well trained and were successful in their careers. So I kept a record of the number of teachers each academic year who were appointed to promoted posts in other schools, helping them with advice, making available plenty of professional development opportunities and, if they wanted it, a mock interview before they went for the real thing. The school lost good staff to other schools but, more importantly, it gained a reputation as a place where good teachers could gain valuable experience, develop professionally, contribute to the development of the

---

5   Times Educational Supplement, 14 August 2015

school and the success of the pupils, and then gain promotion.

School leaders need to avoid the perverse incentives caused by external accountability measures and not let them dictate the nature of their internal accountability systems. By keeping data of the type mentioned above, school leaders can use accountability proactively to monitor the achievement of a school's aims. In this way, accountability is moved from being wholly a feared external process to a leadership tool that can be used positively within the school itself. The school becomes less risk-averse and school leaders pass an explicit message to staff that teaching does not have to be narrow and formulaic.

School governing boards

Governing boards have a key place in the school accountability structure. The governing board holds the head to account, while itself being held to account by Ofsted. When a school is under-performing or in serious financial difficulty, the governing board rightly carries the ultimate responsibility for what has gone wrong.

Heads and governing boards have to work closely if the governing board is to add value to the leadership of the school and exercise accountability in its three key responsibilities – finance, educational standards and strategic planning – as effectively as possible.

For schools in chains and MATs, this depends on a carefully planned scheme of delegation from the board of trustees to the local governing body of the individual schools in the group, so that the maximum responsibility for accountability can lie at the local level, consistent with how well the school is performing. Ultimate accountability remains with the trust board, but successful schools in the trust will have a greater degree of autonomy.

Ofsted inspections

External accountability of schools comes in many different ways – Ofsted inspections, school league tables of test and examination results, threshold measures, floor targets, warning notices, intervention by RSCs and safeguarding regulations, as well as the reputation of the school among parents and the local community. All of these drive policies and practices in schools, sometimes with perverse incentives, as we have seen.

Ofsted inspections cannot any longer be seen in isolation from externally imposed structural change. School leaders fear not only that a set of poor results will bring an Ofsted visit, but also that the RSC will be watching, with consequences for the future of the school. From the school's perspective, the staff and governing body may fear the prospect of an unwelcome sponsor, their single academy forced into a multi-academy trust that it would not choose or their MAT re-brokered to a new group. Yet such change may be needed when a school is doing badly.

The Ofsted inspection framework has gone through many versions, each creating new pressures on school leaders and teachers. It is a process done *to* schools, rather than *with* them. It is too easy for teachers and school leaders to be like rabbits in the headlights of an oncoming train as the time of an inspection approaches, as the system is based on a fundamental lack of trust. As Sir Tim Brighouse has said, *'It is worth reminding ourselves that we are the only developed country with such an elaborate system of school accountability, based essentially on professional mistrust.'* [6]

Prior to the foundation of Ofsted in 1992, inspection had been a rare experience for schools and many teachers went through their whole careers without being inspected.

On 7 January 1984 I received a letter from Her Majesty's Inspectorate informing me that Durham Johnston Comprehensive School would be inspected during the week beginning Monday 15 October. Having not had an inspection for 20 years, the school had nine months to prepare, with the inbuilt danger that staff might think of little else during that time and then collapse in a soggy heap afterwards, as had happened at other schools. I told the staff about the forthcoming inspection, but said to them, *'Your job between now and October is to teach the children as well as you can. I will take care of the preparations for the inspection and let you know when I need information from you.'* Nonetheless, school inspection reports had just started to be published for the first time and it was a high-stakes event, with 20 of Her Majesty's Inspectors (HMIs) in the school for a whole week.

On the Monday evening of the inspection week, we had a reception for the inspectors, welcoming them as fellow professionals who were visiting the school to help us improve. It was a chance for senior staff and governors to meet the inspectors and, interestingly, for the HMIs to meet each other, as many of them had not met before. The inspection was a stressful week, but it was a thorough evaluation of the school and provided some useful learning for the staff. However, it was probably not good value for money to the public purse.

Ofsted inspections have become cheaper, quicker, more tightly focused and much more frequent, but the many changes in the detail of the inspection framework have created a regularly changing set of hoops for schools to jump through. There has often been a worrying lack of consistency among

6   Times Educational Supplement, 21 November 2014

inspectors which, given the high-stakes nature of their judgements, has been unfair on schools; the reputation of some schools has suffered (or been enhanced) unjustifiably. Nonetheless, headteachers taking over the leadership of weak schools have found an adverse inspection to be a useful catalyst for improvement. The end of outsourcing of inspections to commercial companies in 2015 should improve the level of consistency and it is welcome that the use of successful recently retired and serving heads as inspectors has increased.

In the words of the original letter of instructions to inspectors (there were only two of them then) in 1840: *'It is of the utmost consequence you should bear in mind that this inspection is not intended as a means of exercising control, but of affording assistance; that it is not to be regarded as operating for the restraint of local efforts, but for their encouragement; and that its chief objects will not be attained without the cooperation of the school committees; the inspector having no power to interfere, and not being instructed to offer any advice or information except where it is invited.'* [7]

In his biography of Matthew Arnold, his fellow HMI Joshua Fitch reflected that *'the inspector's first duty is to verify the conditions on which public aid is offered to schools and to assure the Department that the nation is obtaining a good equivalent for its outlay. But this is not the whole. He is called upon to visit schools of very different types, to observe the merits and demerits of each ... and to leave behind him at every school some stimulus to improvement.'* [8]

School inspection has a strong tradition of professional independence in England and Wales and, although HM Inspectorate was based within the education department of the government up to the creation of Ofsted in 1992, it has spoken 'without fear or favour' for almost the whole of its existence about both the quality of education in schools and about the success or failure of government policies.

Although the inspectorate may have appeared to have acquired a greater degree of independence as Ofsted, outside the government, it is still statutorily subject to a degree of control by government ministers and this control has been a cause of a great deal of tension at certain times.

The greatest change in 1992, however, was the loss of the professional voice of senior HMIs in the policy-making process in the department, from which the school system has suffered immeasurably since then.

In pursuing a more intelligent accountability system, school leaders will want

---

7   John Dunford, Her Majesty's Inspectorate of schools since 1944: standard bearers or turbulent priests, Woburn Press, 1998, p.2

8   Joshua Fitch, Thomas and Matthew Arnold, Heinemann, 1897

to see inspections that are more clearly focused on just two questions: '*Are the pupils receiving a high quality education?*' and '*Does the school have the capacity to improve?*' The data on attainment and attendance, and compliance issues such as safeguarding, can be dealt with separately. As the former chief inspector, Sir Mike Tomlinson, has said, '*Ofsted has become too data-reliant*'[9], a view shared by many school leaders. Inspections should be data-informed, but not data-driven.

The second of the suggested questions would enable inspectors to make a judgement on the quality of leadership of the school, without that judgement being skewed by other considerations or driven entirely by data.

Quality assurance, peer review and school self-review

In dealing with Ofsted inspections, school leaders have to give a good account of the school's performance within Ofsted's terms of engagement, but not be diverted from the school's own priorities and improvement plan.

This requires school leaders to take control of the accountability agenda, using intelligent accountability internally through school self-review, and using peer review in order to ensure that the school's judgements on its own performance are aligned with the best practice elsewhere.

Annual performance tables and regular Ofsted inspections are forms of *quality control*, whereas good schools seek *quality assurance*, which is a combination of internal self-review and external evaluation, the latter being partly carried out though peer review.

The second pillar of David Miliband's 'new relationship with schools' was '*a simplified school improvement process in which every school uses robust self-evaluation to drive improvement, and ... has access to a dedicated school improvement partner* (SIP) *with whom they conduct a single conversation on targets, priorities and support*'. The network of SIPs was just becoming established in 2010 when Michael Gove abolished SIPs, along with sundry quangos, guidance documents and regulations.

Although Miliband's promotion of self-evaluation and a single conversation on school performance was a move in the right direction, it had by 2010, to some extent, become institutionalised. Like so many government-inspired systems, the standardised self-evaluation form (SEF) had become a bureaucratic exercise for school leaders and the way in which the SEF was used by Ofsted took away from school leaders much of the feeling of ownership of the self-review process.

---

9   Times Educational Supplement, 3 April 2015

However, the quality assurance system that was at the core of the 'new relationship' survived in most schools. Self-review continues to be carried out, without the bureaucratic prop of the standardised SEF, but too often to a pattern dictated by the Ofsted framework.

The external component of accountability has increasingly become peer review, with several schemes offering a thorough, professional evaluation of the progress of the school. For example, Challenge Partners is a growing group of over 300 primary, secondary and special schools, clustered around one of 29 'hub' schools. More than 500 quality assurance (QA) reviews were conducted in partnership schools between 2011 and 2015. In an independent evaluation of the work of Challenge Partners, Matthews and Headon found that the QA reviews have a high degree of credibility in contributing to increased school effectiveness and in developing leadership capacity. Their study found that annual reviews are not mock inspections, but aim to assist the school in checking self-evaluation findings and judging the effectiveness of school improvement strategies.[10]

The Education Development Trust (formerly the CfBT) has its Schools Partnership Programme (SPP), in which there are three components of partnership engagement: self-evaluation, peer review and school-to-school support. Schools work in clusters of three to eight, developing jointly a culture of mutual support and challenge with a rigorous peer review process.

Whole Education offers a peer review service to the schools in its network. This work goes well beyond the scope of an Ofsted inspection, evaluating the extent to which schools offer all learners a fully rounded education, and provides both challenge and support. It captures and evaluates the range of practice being undertaken in network schools. Through these peer reviews, Whole Education reviewers evaluate the ways in which teachers plan, teach and create opportunities to help learners develop wider skills and attributes.

The Channel Islands do not have their own inspectorate, so they use inspectors from England and Scotland to report on the quality of their schools. Each school carries out its own self-review and the role of the inspectors is to validate the school's judgements about its work. This form of peer review has much to commend it, as it incentivises rigorous self-review and tests it against education standards that are wider than the islands' own perspective. It is a system advocated by Sir Tim Brighouse for England.[11] He suggests there should be a

---

10   Peter Matthews and Marcia Headon, Multiple gains: An independent evaluation
      of Challenge Partners' peer reviews of schools, UCL Institute of Education, 2015
11   Times Educational Supplement, 21 November 2014

school self-review framework, supervised by regional bodies responsible for both inspection and school improvement, with the regional body moderating the school's self-review and Ofsted inspecting the regions.

Local accountability

Schools are also accountable to their pupils, parents and indirectly to the local community. There are some excellent examples of student voice being heard in a way that gives young people the opportunity to comment on the performance of the school, feeding into the development of school policies and practices. This aspect of accountability is worth considering in the context of being a 'listening school', which values the opinions of its most important members, the learners.[12]

Parental accountability comes in several different forms, including the mechanism through which parents can complain about a school to Ofsted. It is essential schools take a proactive approach to parent and local accountability. The school website is the obvious vehicle for this, enabling first-hand reports on performance and the full range of the school's activities to be in the public domain – the more data the better to reflect the breadth of the school's activities.

With parent newsletters to draw attention to what is on the website and local newspapers that are nearly always keen to receive copy, there is an opportunity here waiting to be taken. As a head, my rule of thumb was that, since there were bound to be occasions (hopefully rare) when the school got some adverse publicity, and since it takes ten positive news stories to balance one negative piece, I would ensure we got our ten stories in first. My media ambition was to place at least one positive news story about the school in the local paper every week which, with the very small number of journalists employed on the local paper, was not too difficult to achieve.

Professional accountability and trust

The highest form of accountability for professional people such as teachers, however, is the professional accountability to which we hold ourselves. Acting on behalf of the people, the government rightly holds teachers to account, but it is our own view of the extent to which we uphold the highest standards of professionalism that should be our sternest test.

Like Onora O'Neil, we bemoan the lack of trust in us as teachers and school leaders that is implicit in the micro-management and detailed accountability imposed on schools by central government. We recognise that there must be

---

12   See Peacock, op.cit., 2016, chapter 3.

accountability, but we seek a better balance of trust and accountability. This balance surely lies in external accountability that is intelligent, rigorous self-review accepted as a component of the accountability system, and a high level of professional accountability as part of the teaching profession, as much as it is of the legal and medical professions.

***

As public services, it is right that schools are held accountable for their effectiveness and efficiency in the way they spend public money. One has only to consider the lack of accountability at the heart of the newspaper phone-hacking scandal or the way in which the banking system operated to recognise that the public needs accountability as a safeguard. The questions, both for the system as a whole and within schools, are not about whether there should be accountability, but about how much and how. Some would argue there is too much accountability; some would say too little; few would say our accountability system is intelligent in the way that Onora O'Neill defined it.

The aims of schools are broad and confining accountability to a few key measures will almost inevitably narrow the school experience of learners. There is a strong case, therefore, in both external and internal accountability systems, to broaden the range of measures in order to reflect the wider ambitions of schools. Doing this in external systems requires a different approach to inspection and league tables; using a broad range of measures in internal school self-review is an essential component of a high quality education in each institution. Setting the school's own success criteria helps leaders to keep the school on a steady course, avoiding being overwhelmed by frequently changing government performance measures and Ofsted frameworks.

As Onora O'Neill said in her 2002 lectures:

'If we want greater accountability without damaging professional performance we need intelligent accountability. What might this include?

'Let me share my sense of some of the possibilities. Intelligent accountability, I suspect, requires more attention to good governance and fewer fantasies about total control. Good governance is possible only if institutions are allowed some margin for self-governance of a form appropriate to their particular tasks, within a framework of financial and other reporting. Such reporting, I believe, is not improved by being wholly standardised or relentlessly detailed, and since much that has to be accounted for is not easily measured it cannot be boiled down to a set of stock performance indicators. Those who are called to account should give an account of what they have done and of their successes or failures to others who have sufficient time and experience to assess the evidence and report on it. Real

accountability provides substantive and knowledgeable independent judgement of an institution's or professional's work.

'Are we moving towards less distorting forms of accountability? Serious and effective accountability, I believe, needs to concentrate on good governance, on obligations to tell the truth and needs to seek intelligent accountability. I think it has to fantasise much less about Herculean micro-management by means of performance indicators or total transparency. If we want a culture of public service, professionals and public servants must in the end be free to serve the public rather than their paymasters.'

Chapter 6

Leading the education of disadvantaged young people

A nation's greatness is measured by
how it treats its weakest members.
Mahatma Gandhi

Whether it is through the pupil premium in England[1], the pupil deprivation grant in Wales[2] or the Scottish attainment challenge[3], the governments of UK countries are prioritising the closing of the attainment gap between disadvantaged young people and their peers. Responding to these policy initiatives requires an evidence-informed approach from school leaders, who are giving this area a considerable amount of attention, not only because of the accountability for raising the attainment of disadvantaged learners, but because this aspect of school leadership is at the core of their moral purpose and values.

Since 2011, the pupil premium in England has put an increasing amount of funding directly into school budgets to address the needs of disadvantaged

---

1   www.gov.uk/guidance/pupil-premium-information-for-schools-and-alternative-provision-settings

2   gov.wales/topics/educationandskills/schoolshome/deprivation/pdg-and-early-years-pdg/?lang=en

3   www.educationscotland.gov.uk/inclusionandequalities/sac/index.asp

learners. Previous funding boosts, such as excellence in cities or education action zones, were directed at disadvantaged areas, funnelled through local authorities. The London Challenge and its related Challenges in Greater Manchester and the Black Country were regional attempts to close the attainment gap between disadvantaged young people and their peers.

However, many disadvantaged young people do not live in deprived areas, so it is welcome that pupil premium funding in England and Wales is allocated to schools and early years settings for every disadvantaged learner. This has shone a particularly strong light on the performance of disadvantaged learners in rural and suburban areas, for whom schools previously received no additional funding.

There is, of course, no perfect definition of disadvantage. Linking the definition of disadvantage with free school meals (FSM) registration means that some disadvantaged learners fall outside the funding eligibility in England and Wales. The advent of universal free school meals for younger pupils has discouraged some eligible parents from applying for free school meals. The linking of FSM to certain benefits means that some families in quite severe situations of disadvantage and vulnerability are not eligible. Gypsy, Roma and traveller (G/R/T) families, who often operate outside the norms of employment law and the tax system, do not apply for benefits or for FSM, making their children ineligible for pupil premium funding. Primary schools with a high proportion of G/R/T pupils struggle to raise their attainment, battling low attendance, parental illiteracy and the impact of significant cultural differences, with no additional funding. Primary education is often the only schooling many of these children receive, so the schools have to find ways of including these non-FSM children in strategies funded by the pupil premium.

The picture of school achievement by different groups has changed markedly over the last 30 years. While 16 year old Asians did badly in 1970, Chinese, Indian and Bangladeshi children born in 1997-98 did better than any other group. The attainment of White British students has fallen from above average to well below average since 1970.[4] Compared to other countries, the gaps in the UK between the attainment of disadvantaged children and their peers are considerably wider, with countries such as Finland, Singapore and South Korea having, arguably, more homogeneous and egalitarian societies.

Disadvantaged children fall behind their peers from a very young age, so tackling the attainment gap in the early years is critical to success later on. The

---

4   Educational inequalities in England and Wales, Social Market Foundation, 2016
     www.smf.co.uk/wp-content/uploads/2016/01/Publication-Commission-on-
     Inequality-in-Education-Initial-Findings-Slide-Pack-120116.pdf

early years pupil premium was a welcome introduction in 2014, but is paid at a lower rate than the primary or secondary pupil premium and the Education Policy Institute has called for government action to increase the educational quality of childcare and the uptake of the offer for 2 year olds.[5]

Autonomy and accountability for impact

There are few areas of provision in which school leaders have as much autonomy as the decision on how to spend the pupil premium or, in Wales, the pupil deprivation grant (PDG). Put simply, the government gives schools the additional funding, based on their number of disadvantaged learners, and holds them to account for the impact they make with this money on the attainment and progress of these learners. Whether a school has five or 500 learners eligible for additional funding, the same degree of autonomy and accountability applies. What schools do with the money is entirely up to them, but they are held to account for the outcomes.

As we have seen in earlier chapters, teachers have increasingly looked to the government to tell them what to do since 1988, and the government has obliged with a mountain of regulations, advice, guidance and accountability-driven prescription. So it is hardly surprising that, when the government gives schools genuine autonomy to spend the pupil premium, schools look around for advice and, in a worrying number of cases, someone to tell them what to do.

As national pupil premium champion between 2013 and 2015, I did my best to respond to the huge demand for advice, answering direct emails and addressing over 150 meetings and conferences, with a total attendance of around 15,000 teachers, school leaders and governors. However, I invariably prefaced my remarks by saying that I had not come to tell people what policies to adopt in their school, but instead to offer them advice on a strategic approach and evidence to help them decide on the best strategies in their particular circumstances.

Raising attainment and closing the gap

Policies such as pupil premium, the pupil deprivation grant and the Scottish attainment challenge are often referred to as 'closing the gap' policies, but this is only half the story; there are, after all, two ways to close the gap! Indeed, there are several local authority areas with a below-average gap between the attainment of disadvantaged learners and others, not because their disadvantaged pupils are doing so well, but because their more advantaged students are doing so badly.

---

5   Jo Hutchinson and John Dunford, *Divergent pathways: the disadvantage gap, accountability and the pupil premium*, Education Policy Institute, 2016.

Thus, school leaders must prioritise both excellence *and* equity – raising attainment *and* closing the gap. Excellence and raising attainment are pursued because good test and examination results will be a passport to better qualifications, higher education and better jobs. Equity and closing the gap are important because young people who have been dealt a poorer hand in life need extra help from their schools if they are to be successful. Equity means levelling the playing field.

For this reason, school leaders should regard this as a 'raising attainment' agenda, as much as, if not more than, a 'closing the gap' agenda – and thought should be given to what gaps they are trying to close. While it is legitimate to want to close the *in-school gap* between disadvantaged learners and others, it is more challenging for most schools to address the gap between the disadvantaged learners in their school and non-disadvantaged learners *nationally*. Data should be kept on both these gaps.

There are other gaps about which school leaders have concern – the gaps between boys and girls, between summer-born pupils and others, between children with special educational needs and others, between looked-after children and others, between G/R/T children and others, gaps between certain ethnic minorities, or the gap between young people from one part of a school's area and those from elsewhere. While specific funding is not given to schools to close these gaps, school leaders can consider them and spend pupil premium funding in ways that help to raise the attainment of boys, the summer-born, those with special educational needs and others about whom they have concern, who may also have multiple barriers to learning.

It is particularly important to meet the needs of disadvantaged looked-after children. The statistics from 2015 and 2016 tell their own story: [6]

- 68 per cent of looked-after children at age 11 achieved level 4 in reading, compared with 89 per cent of others. The gap is even larger in writing and mathematics.

- 14 per cent of looked-after children achieved 5 or more GCSEs at A*-C, including English and maths, compared with 53 per cent of others.

- 39 per cent of care leavers aged 19-21 are NEET , compared with 13 per cent of all young people.

---

6   NEET is Not in education, employment or training. This data comes from DfE sources, including *Keep on caring*, HMSO, 2016

- 67 per cent of looked-after children have special needs, compared with 18 per cent of the total population.

- 62 per cent of children become looked-after as a result of abuse or neglect and they have a much higher incidence of mental health problems.

Most shocking of all,

- 6 per cent of care leavers go to university, compared with 40 per cent of others, and 4 per cent are in custody.

Looked-after children especially need our additional support to achieve their potential and improve their life chances.

Nor should the needs of bright disadvantaged children be ignored. As the Sutton Trust has found[7], disadvantaged boys are particularly likely to be in the 15 per cent of highly able pupils who score in the top 10 per cent nationally at age 11 but fail to achieve in the top 25 per cent five years later at GCSE. Highly able pupil premium students achieve half a grade less than other highly able pupils, on average, with a very long tail to underachievement. Bright disadvantaged children need additional support, encouragement and aspiration if they are to fulfil their potential.

None of this is easy. Indeed, raising the attainment of disadvantaged learners and closing the gap arguably represent the two greatest challenges for our generation of school leaders. No previous generation of school leaders in the UK has managed substantially to close the gap and, if this can be done using the additional resources now available for this work, the current generation of school leaders will be seen as the best that this country has ever had.

Particularly in the wider social context, the challenge is huge, but the moral imperative compels leaders of every school and early years setting to make their contribution to this vitally important national priority.

Developing a strategy for disadvantaged learners

Barriers to learning

The starting point for developing a strategy for spending the disadvantage funding optimally must be a careful examination of the barriers to learning of these pupils. The reason for having a disadvantage funding stream targeted at individuals is that there is no typical disadvantaged child. All have individual circumstances, which create particular barriers to learning needing different strategies.

---

7   Missing talent, Sutton Trust, 2015 www.suttontrust.com/researcharchive/
      missing-talent/

It is worth spending some time investigating the barriers to learning of individual pupils, so their needs can be addressed in a more targeted way. This can be done through listening to the pupil voice; shadowing one or more disadvantaged learners for a day; data analysis on progress and attendance; learning walks; and talking to parents, staff and governors.

Typically, the following barriers to learning will emerge from such an investigation:

- Lack of support at home
- Low value placed on education by the family
- Lack of engagement of parents/carers with educational progress of their children
- Low aspirations and low expectations, on the part of the family, the learners themselves and, most critical of all to address, members of staff of the school
- Lack of awareness of education, training and employment opportunities
- Limited opportunities outside school, leading to a narrower range of experiences
- Lack of self-confidence and self-esteem
- Poor social and other skills
- Mental and physical health issues, often undiagnosed
- Poor nutrition
- Lack of sleep
- Limited vocabulary
- No support with reading at home and lack of access to books
- Poor attendance
- Poor teaching

There are many more barriers to learning that could be added to this list for some children. There will be other children who are from low socio-economic homes, but who have very supportive families with strong aspirations for their children, who are healthy and have a good diet. One cannot generalise, so the emphasis must be on meeting the needs of individual disadvantaged learners.

A headteacher from Wiltshire asked me a question at a conference which perfectly illustrates the issue here. *'I am executive head of two primary schools,'* he told me, *'and we have put in place exactly the same pupil premium strategies in both schools. Can you explain why they are working well in one school, but are not working in the other?'* My answer was that the children in the two schools are different and may well face different issues. So he needed to investigate the barriers to learning and put in place strategies to address them, responding to individual need as well as raising attainment collectively.

This approach is encapsulated by Ashmount School, an outstanding special school near Loughborough that won a regional pupil premium award in 2014, whose mantra for the spending of its pupil premium is *'Individual need, classroom rigour'* – not a bad mantra for all schools to follow in allocating their pupil premium funding.

Desired outcomes

As with all school policies where funding is being spent, it is important for school leaders to decide, in consultation with staff, governors, parents and learners, on the objectives of their pupil premium expenditure. Having identified the barriers to learning of their disadvantaged pupils, school leaders and governors will want to set out what they hope to achieve in helping the learners to overcome these barriers. For additional spending on disadvantaged learners, the desired outcomes might be as follows:

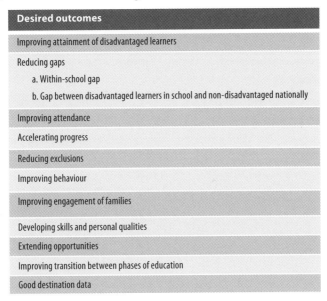

Desired outcomes
Improving attainment of disadvantaged learners
Reducing gaps
a. Within-school gap
b. Gap between disadvantaged learners in school and non-disadvantaged nationally
Improving attendance
Accelerating progress
Reducing exclusions
Improving behaviour
Improving engagement of families
Developing skills and personal qualities
Extending opportunities
Improving transition between phases of education
Good destination data

Figure 3

'Good destination data' applies to secondary schools; all other desired outcomes could be used by schools of any type in any phase of education.

This is not intended to be a definitive list. Some schools will delete items inappropriate for them; other schools will want to add desired outcomes.

Success criteria and accountability

It is not sufficient for school leaders to set out the aims of the school for its disadvantaged learners. For each of these desired outcomes, it is also important for school leaders and governors to define what success looks like, in order to be able to evaluate policies and know whether they are achieving what the school intends. These success criteria can be put into a second column on the table, as follows:

Desired outcomes	Success criteria
Improving attainment of disadvantaged learners	Improve attainment of disadvantaged learners from x% in 2016 to y% in 2017 to z% in 2018
Reducing gaps a. Within-school gap b. Gap between disadvantaged learners in school and non-disadvantaged nationally	
Improving attendance	
Accelerating progress	Every disadvantaged learner makes at least good progress every half-term
Reducing exclusions	
Improving behaviour	
Improving engagement of families	
Developing skills and personal qualities	
Extending opportunities	On the school's list of opportunities, increase the number accessed by disadvantaged learners from x to y
Improving transition between phases of education	Statistics generated by surveys of pupils and parents in years 6, 7 and 8 reveal an improving picture
Good destination data	a. Increase the proportion of disadvantaged students gaining places at Russell Group universities from p to q b. No disadvantaged students becoming NEET in the year after leaving school

Figure 4

I have inserted five examples of possible success criteria and how they might be defined, but every school will have its own success criteria – and this is an important component of school leadership in this field. These success criteria are not being set for the school by the government or by Ofsted; they are decided and monitored by the school itself. In other words, school leaders are taking ownership of accountability for their success in improving the life chances of disadvantaged learners – a concrete example of the proactive approach to accountability discussed in the previous chapter.

This is empowering for the school and helps to put a tough edge on the moral purpose of school leaders and teachers to do their best for the disadvantaged. It encapsulates the pursuit of both excellence and equity.

However, the moral purpose of school leadership for the benefit of young people from deprived backgrounds cannot be described simply by a set of statistics in the column of a table. Turning around the sometimes chaotic lives of these children is much more complex and important than that.

So, along with the success criteria and the statistics, it is good to write up some case studies of individual children, explaining how the pupil premium has been used to improve their readiness for learning and their life chances. If a case study can be completely anonymised, it can be put on the school's website as part of the pupil premium report; if not, the case study can be kept in the school's own accountability file. Either way, it speaks volumes about the ethos of the school.

Only when the barriers to learning have been thoroughly investigated, desired outcomes set out and success criteria agreed, is the school leadership in a position to decide what strategies to use in order to achieve the success criteria.

Choosing the right strategies

When the pupil premium was introduced in England in 2011, schools used the funding partly to pay for things they were doing anyway, as well as to take on more teaching assistants for individual tuition and classroom support, and to subsidise school trips. According to an Ofsted survey in 2012, however, schools mostly did not have any specific plan as to how these strategies would improve the progress and attainment of disadvantaged learners.[8]

During the following five years, however, schools have begun to target their pupil premium funding much more clearly, using evidence to select the most effective strategies. Thus, support for literacy or maths is better focused and is often done by qualified teachers or highly trained teaching assistants; tracking of progress is directed particularly strongly at disadvantaged pupils, with data monitored frequently and rapid interventions made where required; social and emotional support is given where needed; additional activities are subsidised,

---

8   Ofsted, The pupil premium: how schools used the funding, HMSO, September 2012, www.gov.uk/government/publications/the-pupil-premium-how-schools-used-the-funding

in a way that is better targeted at raising attainment; funding is spent on ways of improving attendance; and the specific needs of individual learners are analysed and met.

As has been discussed in earlier chapters, many schools have become risk-averse and have tended to put in place what they have been told by central government or what they perceive will gain the school a good Ofsted grade at their next inspection. The way in which the pupil premium is allocated to schools directly, with accountability for impact, has given school leaders immense opportunities for innovation. As I learned during my two years as national pupil premium champion, visiting almost all areas of England, many schools have been extremely creative in their use of the funding. Some examples are seen below:

Examples of innovative practice in the use of the pupil premium

1. A secondary school in London found that its disadvantaged students were more often absent or late than others, so it purchased alarm clocks for them.

2. The national winner of the pupil premium awards in 2015, the Ark Charter Academy in Portsmouth, had an acute problem of attendance among its disadvantaged students. It introduced several strategies to improve attendance, including the leasing of a minibus to go round the area and collect absentees.

3. Some schools keep back a proportion of the pupil premium grant and invite staff to bid for this money for projects to help disadvantaged learners.

4. Staff in quite a few schools have agreed that, when they mark a set of exercise books, they will mark the books of pupil premium learners first.

5. Many schools have used the funding to lease musical instruments and pay for music tuition for disadvantaged learners. For example, drums were the chosen instrument for a boy in South Gloucestershire, who reported that this had improved his co-ordination and hence his handwriting.

6. A primary school in the north-east pays for every disadvantaged learner to attend the theatre every year.

7. Using pupil premium funding to respond to individual need: weight watchers classes for an obese child; a wig for a girl with alopecia; expenses associated with being members of the sea scouts, boy scouts, girl guides and the Duke of Edinburgh award; expenses to attend a football academy of excellence, which increased the self-esteem of an 11 year old and thus improved his attendance.

8. A group of parents at a primary school in Wiltshire had difficulty engaging with their children's education, as their own literacy levels were so low. The school used pupil premium funding to pay for these parents to attend literacy classes at the local college.

9. Imaginative ways to get parents into school who would normally be reluctant to come in, such as a bake-off competition.

10. Many schools pay for free breakfasts for disadvantaged learners; some invite the parents of these children to have a free breakfast with them and use the opportunity for informal conversation about education and the progress of the learner.

One of the barriers to learning of many disadvantaged learners is the narrowness of their experience outside school and the lack of opportunities they have to gain experiences that their more fortunate peers take for granted – going to the theatre, visiting the seaside, holidaying abroad, or spending a day in the countryside. When teaching in a secondary school on a large housing estate north of the River Wear in Sunderland, I was astonished to learn that some of the pupils had never been into Sunderland and had no idea how far it was to Newcastle. The narrowness of their lives was a major barrier to their education and their ambition.

The narrowness of their cultural experience also has a huge impact on their vocabulary, which in turn impacts on their progress in reading comprehension. This affects so much of their learning. It can also directly affect their test scores, such as in the 2016 Key Stage 2 reading test, which included a text based on colonial Africa, full of vocabulary well beyond the experience of many British 11 year olds. An inner city Manchester primary school, with a high percentage of disadvantaged learners, has established an innovative programme of planned visits, linked to texts and carefully planned vocabulary learning, from early years through to age 11. It includes a journey on a bus into central Manchester, a local walk to learn the vocabulary of street furniture, visits to farms, a zoo and the beach.

The National Trust has a list of *50 things to do before you are 11¾* and it is highly likely that, if schools use this as a survey of their 11 year olds, the disadvantaged children will have done fewer of the activities than their better-off peers.[9] However, this is a list of rural activities – dam a stream, camp out in the wild, make a home for a wild animal – that aims to get children out into the countryside, which is only part of what schools want to do to broaden the experience of disadvantaged children. Many schools have used the principle behind the National Trust list, but have produced their own list of 30, 40 or 50 activities and have then set out to give the pupils the opportunities to do these things within the context of the broader curriculum discussed in chapter 3.

Using evidence

Making an impact with pupil premium funding depends on targeting the needs of individuals and making good use of data. School leaders now understand much more clearly where they can access evidence of what is working elsewhere and are more prepared to use their autonomy to put in place strategies that will help to achieve their success criteria.

Teachers have historically been weak at using evidence to inform their practice. This is partly because research evidence is more contested in education than in, say, medicine, where patients would be very unhappy with doctors or dentists who did not keep up to date with the latest developments. It is also because teachers have had no equivalent of *The Lancet* or the *British Medical Journal*, although the government has said in the 2016 White Paper that it will fund such a publication to make peer-reviewed research more accessible to teachers.

Disadvantage funding offers an excellent opportunity to school leaders to use evidence on strategies for supporting disadvantaged learners, since this evidence is readily available to teachers, notably in three places.

First, the Education Endowment Foundation (EEF) toolkit[10], which is based on an analysis by Durham University of 10,000 research projects worldwide, is an accessible database that summarises the effectiveness of 30 or so strategies. For each strategy there is an estimate of the relative cost of implementation, a grade according to the depth of research evidence, and a figure for the likely months of impact on pupil progress. Behind each strategy is a page summarising how to implement the intervention successfully, recent studies on the topic, the likely costs per learner of implementation, related research projects, and what school leaders need to consider if they decide to adopt the strategy.

---

9   www.50things.org.uk
10   educationendowmentfoundation.org.uk/evidence/teaching-learning-toolkit/

The EEF toolkit is an excellent place to seek evidence of high-impact, low-cost strategies and to decide which of these might best meet the needs of an individual school.

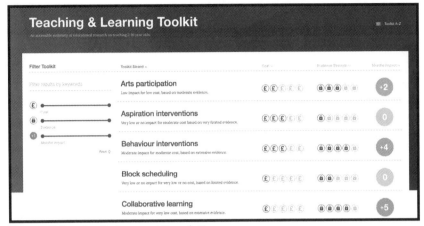

Figure 5 Education Endowment Foundation

There is a parallel early years toolkit, which provides evidence for the most effective use of the early years pupil premium.

For school leaders who wish to carry out research, there is no better opportunity than to participate in an EEF research project on a specific aspect of their work with disadvantaged learners, usually through randomised control trials.

The government in Wales has published advice for its schools on the evidence of successful practice in using the pupil deprivation grant.[11]

The second source of evidence on successful practice is to seek out what is working well in schools that have been successful in raising the attainment of disadvantaged learners and closing the gap. Each year since 2013, the DfE has given regional and national awards for work with the pupil premium. The pupil premium awards website[12] lists all the winners and includes some case studies.

Every school in England is statutorily obliged to have a pupil premium section on its website and this provides a wealth of evidence for schools investigating excellent practice. The websites of the schools that have won pupil premium awards make a good starting point for this search. In addition, the EEF Families

---

11   learning.gov.wales/docs/learningwales/publications/140512-what-really-works-en.pdf

12   www.pupilpremiumawards.co.uk

of Schools database[13] provides data on every school in comparison with the 50 schools that most closely resemble it in socio-economic composition.

Marc Rowland of the National Education Trust has visited over 150 primary, special and secondary schools, looking at their pupil premium practice and conducting reviews, and his practical guide is a useful resource of good practice across the country in a wide range of types of school.[14]

The third source of evidence on successful practice is published reports on pupil premium in England.

- Ofsted has produced three reports on pupil premium and the second of these, published in 2013, followed a survey of schools and contains a useful list of successful, and less successful, approaches to the use of the funding.[15]

- A report from the National Foundation for Education Research in 2015[16] surveyed the use of the pupil premium in a range of schools, concluding that there were seven 'building blocks of success'.

- At the end of my two years as national pupil premium champion in August 2015, I wrote a blog post[17] summarising the lessons I had learned during that time about the most successful strategies and interventions being used by schools.

I have brought these three sources together in a single list, which school leaders may find useful as a checklist on practice in their own schools in relation to disadvantaged learners:

---

13 educationendowmentfoundation.org.uk/attainment-gap/families-of-schools-database/

14 Marc Rowland, An updated practical guide to the pupil premium, John Catt Publications, second edition, 2015

15 Ofsted, The pupil premium: How schools are spending the funding successfully to maximise achievement, HMSO, 2013 www.gov.uk/government/publications/the-pupil-premium-how-schools-are-spending-the-funding-successfully

16 Shona Macleod, Caroline Sharp, Daniele Bernardinelli et al, Supporting the attainment of disadvantaged pupils: Articulating success and good practice: Research Report, November 2015 www.nfer.ac.uk/publications/PUPP01

17 johndunfordconsulting.co.uk/blog/

The building blocks of success in schools where disadvantaged pupils have high achievement:

School culture

Ethos of attainment for all pupils

Unerring **focus on high quality teaching**

Clear, responsive leadership, with high aspirations and expectations

100 per cent buy-in from all staff, with all staff conveying positive and aspirational messages to disadvantaged pupils

Evidence (especially the EEF Toolkit) is used to decide on which strategies are likely to be most effective in overcoming the barriers to learning of disadvantaged pupils. Particular consideration is given to high-impact, low-cost strategies.

Ability to demonstrate positive **impact** of all strategies

In-depth training for all staff on chosen strategies

Every effort is made to **engage parents/ carers** in the education and progress of their child

Individual support

Identification of the main **barriers to learning** for disadvantaged pupils

Individualised approach to addressing barriers to learning and emotional support

Focus on outcomes for all individual pupils

Frequent monitoring of the progress of every disadvantaged pupil

When a pupil's progress slows, **interventions** are put in place rapidly

Teachers know **which pupils are eligible** for pupil premium

The needs are recognised of disadvantaged children in **specific groups**, e.g. high ability pupils, looked-after children

School organisation

Deployment of the best staff to support disadvantaged pupils – developing the skills of existing teachers and teaching assistants

Excellent collection, analysis and use of **data** relating to individual pupils and groups

115

> **Performance management** is used to reinforce the importance of this agenda
>
> **Effectiveness of teaching assistants** is evaluated and, if necessary, improved through training and better deployment
>
> **Governors** are trained on pupil premium
>
> **Pupil premium funding is ring-fenced** to spend on the target group
>
> **Effectiveness of interventions is evaluated frequently** and adjustments made as necessary
>
> **A senior leader has oversight** of how pupil premium funding is being spent

All three of the sources used in constructing the above list include the quality of teaching as a significant factor. School leaders will find it useful to draw on evidence for this, which can be found in a Sutton Trust report of 2011[18] and is illustrated in the diagram below.

Effect of teaching on students in years of progress

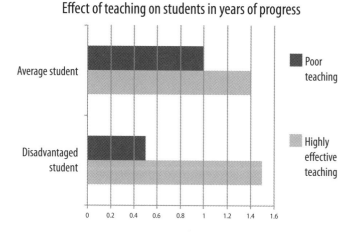

Figure 6 Sutton Trust, 2011

Poor teaching hampers the progress of disadvantaged students, on average, by six months per year, disproportionately holding back these learners, and is therefore a major contributory factor in the gap that exists between the attainment of disadvantaged learners and others. Fortunately, the evidence also

---

18   Improving the impact of teachers on pupil achievement in the UK, Sutton Trust, 2011 www.suttontrust.com/wp-content/uploads/2011/09/2teachers-impact-report-final.pdf

shows that excellent teaching disproportionately helps disadvantaged learners. The elimination of poor teaching and the provision of excellent teaching for disadvantaged students are therefore vitally important components of the pupil premium strategy of all schools. Since raising the quality of teaching both increases attainment and helps to close the gap, it is legitimate to spend pupil premium funding on improving teaching quality.

Evaluation

Babington Community College in Leicester, which won the East Midlands pupil premium award in 2013, lists 48 different strategies on which it spends its pupil premium funding of just over £400,000. For the school principal, Denise Newsome, and the vice-principal, Sara Fletcher, spending the pupil premium effectively and efficiently is vitally important if they are to translate the additional funding into impact on the attainment of disadvantaged learners. With a gap of only 2 per cent between the results of disadvantaged 16 year olds and others, they are certainly successful and an important reason for this is the way in which the senior leadership team of the school, and Sara Fletcher as the pupil premium lead, frequently evaluate the impact of each of their strategies. If any strategy is not delivering its intended impact, it is dropped immediately and the funding is spent on something that the school's leaders judge likely to be more effective.

School self-evaluation was discussed in chapter 5 and schools such as Babington are using it to particularly good effect in constantly improving the impact of their work with disadvantaged learners.

External pupil premium reviews on a school can be ordered by Ofsted after an inspection, but more commonly external reviews are commissioned by the school itself. In the early years of the pupil premium, the quality of these reviews was variable and so the Teaching Schools Council published a guide, a second edition of which was published in 2016.[19] This has been written in a way that the methodology can be used for both external and internal reviews.

A second tool that can be used for evaluation of pupil premium policy is the EEF's Families of Schools Database, mentioned above (See figure 7). This database does not require a login and is very easy to use, offering school leaders the opportunity to see which similar schools are doing best, after which their websites can be visited and contact made with the headteacher or pupil premium co-ordinator to discuss their strategies. While successful strategies in

---

19   Effective pupil premium reviews, Teaching Schools Council, 2016
     tscouncil.org.uk/resources/guide-to-effective-pupil-premium-reviews/

one school may not work well in another, as we have seen, the database opens a door on best practice and this can be fed by school leaders into the evaluation of the strategies in their own school.

The Families of Schools Database

Education
Endowment
Foundation

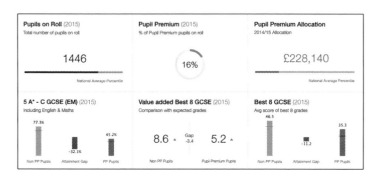

Figure 7 Education Endowment Foundation

Role of governors

It is essential that school leaders involve governors in decisions about pupil premium expenditure and keep them informed about progress towards the success criteria that they will have agreed. The reason for this is straightforward: raising attainment of disadvantaged learners and closing the gap should be key parts of the school development plan, which is agreed and owned by the governing body.

Knowing what questions to ask the head and senior staff is important for governors. In order to make their decisions about pupil premium effectively and fulfil their accountability function, governors need to be fully informed about pupil premium and related policies, and may well want to ask the headteacher questions such as these:

- How many pupils are eligible for pupil premium?
- How much additional funding does the school receive?
- How is this funding allocated?
- How is the school evaluating the impact it is making with the funding?
- What progress is being made each term by disadvantaged learners? How

does this compare with progress made by other pupils?

- How is the school improving the engagement of the parents of disadvantaged learners?
- What interventions are helping bright disadvantaged children to achieve their potential?
- What interventions are helping looked-after children to raise their attainment?

At the end of the year,

- On all measures, what was the attainment of pupils eligible for pupil premium, compared with the attainment of other pupils?
- How does the school's pupil premium data compare with national data for non-pupil premium students?

Using curriculum to help close the gap

The curriculum can make a substantial contribution to the life chances of learners from disadvantaged homes. Many of these children start school with multiple barriers to learning. In addition to spending additional funding on overcoming these barriers, the design of the curriculum can help to close the gap between these children and others.

In the early years, an emphasis on literacy, vocabulary and reading will have disproportionate benefit for children who have had less exposure to books and conversation in the first years of their lives.

St Mary's Church of England Primary School is in a disadvantaged part of Southampton and the school recognises clearly the barriers that the pupils need to overcome if they are to have a good start to their education. On the wall in the school entrance area, which is visited by many parents, the curriculum for each year is posted, including both the knowledge and skills that are to be learned in each year. This curriculum indicates that the school is giving its pupils a whole education of the sort described in chapter 3.

Because disadvantaged children have less opportunity to develop skills and attributes outside school, it is particularly important that the curriculum includes plans to develop these characteristics. All children will develop skills during their school years, so it is incumbent on school leaders to plan a skills development programme in order to ensure that the skills taught in the classroom are the ones that will most benefit the young people.

This balance of knowledge, skills and attributes can be continued in the curriculum – defined in its broadest terms, as in chapter 3 – through all of primary and secondary education, with the co-curriculum playing an important role in broadening the range of experiences of disadvantaged learners.

It is particularly important to have a full range of options at Key Stage 4 and not to narrow the curriculum to an EBacc diet if the maximum potential is to be drawn from young people from disadvantaged backgrounds. It is as desirable for a secondary school to have as an objective that none of its disadvantaged students will become NEET in the year after leaving as it is to set a target for the number gaining places at Russell Group universities – and both of those objectives place particular demands on curriculum planning.

Whole Education Network schools operate in the belief that it will only be through the commitment to an entitlement to a whole education for all that any school or system will truly narrow the gap and make a real difference to the life chances of all young people.

***

Few aspects of school leadership are so rooted in values and moral purpose as the education of learners from disadvantaged backgrounds. I am sure that that is the reason why I had such a good reception from so many people during my two years as national pupil premium champion. With the methodology outlined above, careful use of the evidence available on what works, and an innovative approach, school leaders can make more of a difference in this area than in almost any other.

This may be the greatest challenge for our generation of school leaders, but it is the aspect of school leadership that can bring the greatest reward.

Chapter 7

Watering the plants: leading a learning school

Who dares to teach, must never cease to learn.
John Cotton Dana, New Jersey, 1912

Leadership and learning are indispensable to each other.
John F Kennedy

A learning school is one where everyone is a learner, from the headteacher to the youngest pupil. In a learning community, it should be unthinkable that anyone might not put learning at the centre of their work, so it should be a priority for every member of the teaching and support staff to continue to be a learner, with senior leaders creating the climate for this and setting an example through their own learning.

Watering the plants

When I was appointed as a head, I told the appointment committee that it was my job to water the plants. My predecessor had been an autocrat (it was said that his catchphrase was 'no') and I needed to nurture the staff and get them thinking about the job and taking real responsibility, not just passing decisions upwards as they had grown accustomed to doing.

There are teachers – and there turned out to be several of them in the school when I took up headship – who considered that their 20 years' experience fully equipped them for their teaching. In reality, many of them had had one year's experience 20 times and, although they did not recognise it, were in desperate need of professional refreshment.

There is now evidence of the importance of leading professional development as the top priority activity for school leaders of successful schools – 'watering the plants' is better grounded in research than I could have imagined at the time I said it, although not all academics agree with the legitimacy of the conclusion that 'leading teacher learning and development' has an effect size of 0.84.[1]

Five Dimensions of Student-Centred Leadership

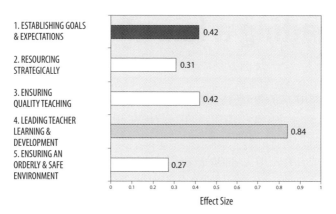

Figure 8 Dimensions of student-centred leadership[2]

Viviane Robinson's research gives objective support to the subjective view that nothing is more important for school leaders than encouraging and incentivising staff to engage in professional development which improves the quality of teaching. As school leaders reflect on the myriad policies described in the earlier chapters of this book, they wonder time and again why education ministers miss the central point that the quality of teaching is the most significant factor in improving the life chances of young people.

1   See Dylan Wiliam, Leadership for teacher learning: creating a culture where all teachers improve so that all students succeed, Abe Books, 2016; and Gary Jones, 'When the evidence is not all that it seems and the case of the 0.84 effect size for leading teaching learning and development', 2016 at evidencebasededucationalleadership.blogspot.co.uk/2016/07/when-evidence-is-not-all-that-it-seems.html

2   Viviane Robinson, Student-centred leadership, Wiley, 2011

While millions of pounds are spent on free schools where there is no shortage of places or on lawyers and consultants to support schools converting to academy status, many schools are economising on professional development. This puts at risk the improvement journey of the school and limits staff opportunities, when professional development could be the most cost-effective way through which the school could improve.

A small amount of money can go a long way if the quality of the professional development is good – a day spent visiting an excellent school, a week spent doing a small-scale research project on a high-priority topic for the school's development plan, the purchase of high-quality resources to be used by a group of staff to improve the teaching of literacy, or a good staff research library, for example.

At a time of budgetary constraint, cost-free professional development might have a role to play – better focused staff and sectional meetings, or the transfer of expertise from one teacher to another. At Durham Johnston School, the first few staff training days in the 1980s did not go well. These were known then as 'Baker days', mainly so staff could mentally stick pins into an effigy of Kenneth Baker who had, they considered, deprived them of five days of holiday per year. Speakers with national reputations came up to Durham to speak to the staff and too often went down like a balloon in a box of nails. The turning point came when we realised we had the self-confidence to use our own staff, instead of visiting experts, in training leadership roles. Thirty years later, I can still recall the first day we did this, with all staff attending four lessons given by other teachers, who had volunteered to be observed, and experiencing outstanding teaching in subjects other than their own. We were a much stronger team as a result.

Changing the culture: 'Look outwards, not upwards'

The teaching profession has spent over 20 years in a suffocating centrally-directed policy climate, in which governments have told heads and teachers what to do and, increasingly, how to do it. This has created a culture in which school leaders and teachers have grown accustomed to looking upwards to see what they are being told to do.

Since 2010, the government has made it a policy priority to give more freedom to schools, although, as we have seen in earlier chapters, curriculum, examinations and accountability drivers are still creating major constraints. Especially in risk-averse schools, there is a big temptation to let these constraints dictate policies and practices and not to use the available freedoms.

More confident schools, however, have taken the government at its word and used the freedoms available to them to translate their vision and values into policy and practice. Underpinning much of the work I have done in recent years, supporting school improvement and disseminating good practice with the pupil premium, has been the message that, if government ministers are saying that schools and teachers should have more freedom, let us take them at their word: *Stop looking up and start looking out* to the many amazing projects and ideas that are happening elsewhere and to the best evidence available of effective practice.

In many schools, this requires a culture change. For too many teachers, their classroom is the boundary of their experience. If they have any spirit of enquiry, it is scarcely evident in their professional practice and school leaders have to work hard to move these staff into a more developmental approach to their work. For other schools, where the culture is more outward-looking, the challenge is to provide the opportunities for staff to meet their professional development needs and align those with the aims of the school.

Never has there been so much evidence available from good educational research on classroom practice and school improvement. From John Hattie's meta-analysis of hundreds of research projects[3] to the EEF's toolkit and its research projects, this evidence is now much more accessible than it has been in the past. There is some excellent work from academics such as Andy Hargreaves, David Hargreaves, Michael Fullan and Guy Claxton, and the papers published by groups such as the Sutton Trust, Policy Exchange and the Education Policy Institute provide school leaders with an immense amount of accessible material to inform their decision-making and to bring to the attention of their staff. Long gone are the days when professional development meant solely attending one-day courses. These still have their place – and were a very useful means of dissemination in my work as national pupil premium champion – but only in the context of a wider professional development plan.

Building a strong professional development community

In being a proactive school leader, making the most of the opportunities available to innovate and chart a well-defined course for the school, the building of a strong professional community that encourages the sharing of excellent practice is a high priority. At a time of pressure on school budgets, when many schools reduce the professional development budget before anything else, determined leadership is vital to maintain a developmental ethos. Working in a cost-effective and time-effective way, there are six measures that can be taken to support staff in playing an active learning role:

---

3   John Hattie, Visible learning, Routledge, 2009

1. Promote a climate of learning by setting an example

2. Appoint a senior member of staff to oversee professional development and include research in his/her brief, either in an individual school or across a group of schools

3. Join a local teaching school alliance and make the most of the development opportunities offered by the alliance

4. Encourage staff to participate in local and national networks and to join with staff in other schools on developmental work in their fields of activity

5. Filter research evidence, so staff do not have to sift through hundreds of pages that will be of little or no help to them; make this evidence readily available in the school

6. Become a school member of the Teacher Development Trust[4] and use its database of high quality professional development providers before signing up for training opportunities

Promoting a climate of learning means that the senior leaders in the school must set an example, whether doing a PhD or a Master's degree, or bringing back to the staff the lessons learned from research, from available evidence, from courses or conferences they have attended, or from external contacts with other schools and researchers. In particular, the head should be a role model of learning.

Appointing a senior member of staff to oversee professional development and research is helpful. In allocating the responsibilities of the senior team, the values and priorities of the school are reflected. While the creation of a culture of professional learning, with all members of staff taking responsibility for their own development, is an essential goal, there still has to be a senior co-ordinating figure to ensure that professional development is aligned with school development priorities and that the full breadth of the range of opportunities is brought to the attention of all staff. Joint practice development with other schools is unlikely to take place unless it is encouraged and facilitated from the top. It is logical for this member of the leadership team also to be in charge of research at the school, tying staff research interests with the needs of the school. This role can be particularly influential when it is held across a group of schools, for example in a multi-academy trust.

At Huntington School, York, Alex Quigley is director of learning and research. The Huntington head, John Tomsett, believes that teaching will only become

---

4   www.tdtrust.org

an evidence-informed profession if school leaders create the conditions where classroom teachers can access research easily; feel encouraged to change practice in the light of evidence; are supported by a research lead in the school with a connection to higher education; and can evaluate the impact on student outcomes of changes to their pedagogy.

Joining a local teaching school alliance sends a positive message to staff and increases opportunities for professional development at all levels. Especially for schools trying to build their professional development from a low base, teaching schools provide a wide range of opportunities for staff to gain experience from beyond their own school and expand their learning.

Encouraging staff to participate in local and national networks can broaden horizons. As a maths teacher, I found meetings of the local maths group to be a very useful learning experience. Whether local networks are organised by a teaching school, the local authority, subject associations or a group of enterprising teachers, they can be invaluable in bringing teachers into contact with others.

There are plenty of national networks, which are easy to access in the first instance through websites and social media. Subject associations and organisations such as Whole Education and the National Education Trust are professional learning communities that provide invaluable and stimulating contact between teachers from different parts of the country.

Making research evidence available to staff in a manageable way helps to nurture professional development. Much education research has previously been published more for the benefit of the researchers than for teachers. Written in specialist language and published in obscure journals that never find their way into schools, most research has had little practical benefit for children's education. In the absence of an educational equivalent of *The Lancet*, there are research summary services, such as that produced by the School of Education at the University of Bristol, to which schools can subscribe.[5] The EEF toolkit forms the most user-friendly research tool, gleaning evidence from over 10,000 studies of strategies that work most effectively – and most cost-effectively – on school improvement, especially in raising the attainment of disadvantaged learners. EEF research projects, based in schools, are also written up in an accessible way.

Ensuring that staff attend only high quality professional development courses is part of the role of the senior leader with oversight of professional development.

5   Document summary service, School of Education, University of Bristol
     edn.bris.ac.uk/dss/

Historically, there has been wide variation in the quality of external courses and the Teacher Development Trust has been formed partly to raise the quality of provision. Its TDT Advisor tool is free to use and provides a list of the best professional development resources – courses, conferences, consultancy services, printed and online material. In the manner of TripAdvisor, teachers can comment on the quality of training and resources. In addition to user comments, professional development provision is subject to random audits by the Teacher Development Trust and providers have to sign up to a code of practice.

Sarah Coskeran of the Trust has set out four tests of good CPD[6], which teachers are advised to follow before committing to a professional development activity:

- Where is the evidence that this activity will help me and my students?
- What follow-up and support are on offer?
- Will the training help to evaluate its impact?
- You say you're good – but who can corroborate your quality?

Being part of a wider professional development community

In a school that is part of a wider professional development community, such as a teaching school or a MAT, the views of experts are heard and discussed; pockets of good practice in each school are shared; research is accessed and evaluated; innovations expand teachers' thinking; information gathered is considered in the context of teachers' own schools; and evidence-informed policy is introduced, with teachers able to compare the impact in their different situations.

A spectrum of professional development

The rapid growth in the number of teaching school alliances, now covering nearly all the country, has thrown the responsibility for leading professional development and leadership development into the hands of excellent schools, which is exactly where it should be.

Between 2013 and 2015 I was part of a research team carrying out an evaluation of the work of teaching schools[7] and had the privilege of visiting in each of the three years Portswood Teaching School in Southampton, the Cambridge Teaching Schools Network and the South Lakes Federation in Cumbria. Government policy on teaching schools is sufficiently flexible for

---

6   'The four tests of good CPD for your school', SecEd, 14 November 2013

7   Qing Gu et al, Teaching schools evaluation: final report, National College for Teaching and Leadership, 2015 www.gov.uk/government/publications/teaching-schools-evaluation-final-research-report. Case studies of teaching schools, including the ones mentioned here, are at tscouncil.org.uk/the-work-of-teaching-schools-and-their-alliances/

the three teaching schools to be constructed and managed in different ways. Portswood has spread outwards from an excellent primary school that had long been involved in school improvement work; the Cambridge Network is led by five excellent schools forming three teaching schools but working as a single network; and the South Lakes Federation extended a partnership that had grown out of the needs of that rural area to work together on 14-19 education. The report's findings have some useful lessons for schools expanding their professional development work, with teaching schools increasingly collaborating across their localities.

Many teaching schools are building a spectrum of professional development, from initial teacher education through newly qualified teachers and second year support, to CPD for serving teachers, middle and senior leadership development and networks for executive headship. The evaluation report found that the schools regarded professional development as the main strength of their offer to schools in their alliance.

Although the report found that the experience of working in a teaching school alliance gives staff more opportunity to develop their leadership beyond their own school, the professional development and leadership development tend mostly to be in the form of short courses and are not yet well linked to research work or to joint practice development (JPD) with other schools.

Nonetheless, teaching schools provide many opportunities for leadership at all stages of the spectrum of training and development, and are particularly good for giving leadership experience beyond their own school to talented members of staff.

Initial Teacher Training (ITT)

Half of teachers in training are on higher education courses, with the other half in schools, either with school-centred ITT providers (SCITTs) or on School Direct, delivered by teaching school alliances. Teach First, which I have supported from its inception and whose board I was on for several years, accounts for about 6 per cent of trainees. Planning of teacher numbers, which the TDA (Training and Development Agency for Schools) used to do with a degree of success, has largely disappeared, contributing to shortages in 2016 in all subjects in secondary education, except English, history and physical education. Over-recruitment to primary for 2016 contrasts with secondary, which filled only around 80 per cent of places.

School leaders have a big role to play in teacher training, although School Direct has involved an enormous amount of additional work for the leaders of teaching schools. There is merit in schools taking the lead in initial training but, in a national service such as education with nearly half a million teachers, it is essential that this is done to profession-led national standards and that numbers are planned nationally, regionally and by sector, with incentives in shortage subjects and national recruitment strategies.

Retention first, recruitment second

Recruitment would be easier if retention were better, but the retention statistics indicate that there is a major problem to be addressed. 25 per cent of state school teachers leave before they have spent five years in the job, with 106,000 qualified teachers under 60 never having taught in a state school. Over 40,000 teachers leave the profession each year – an annual wastage rate of around 10 per cent.[8]

The reasons for poor retention statistics are not hard to find, with surveys of teachers frequently citing workload, pupil behaviour, the nature of the accountability regime and constant government-imposed change. While some of this is undoubtedly the fault of the government, and denigration of teachers in the media may be a factor too, there is much school leaders can do to improve retention.

Expecting teachers to work hard is not, in itself, a problem. The workload issue has more to do with the lack of control that many teachers feel over their work, and school leaders can do something about that. Creating and maintaining an upbeat, innovative climate in which the views of staff are genuinely taken into account is a major contributor to retention, as is the minimising of bureaucratic demands on staff. Encouraging strong teamwork, so that no staff feel isolated or unsupported, is critical. If teachers feel they are being made by school leaders to jump through hoops, completing over-detailed lesson plans and endless preparation for performance management and Ofsted inspections, they are unlikely to be positive about their job. Good retention figures should be included in every school leader's personal accountability portfolio.

Talent management and succession planning

Another main strand of teaching school work is talent management and succession planning, with teaching schools – and alliance schools that are working most closely with them – identifying especially talented staff early in their careers and providing them with planned opportunities to develop rapidly into middle and senior leaders. In places where recruitment to senior positions is difficult, this is a great benefit for schools at the core of teaching school alliances.

---

8   Department for Education, School workforce survey, 2014

Whether in a teaching school alliance or not, it is an important part of school leadership to nurture the next generation of leaders. Many heads, including me, can recall particular points in their career when their headteacher gave them an opportunity that provided useful leadership experience. One of my proudest achievements as a head was that six Durham Johnston teachers subsequently became heads themselves, and many more have joined school leadership teams.

Engagement in research

Professors of medicine carry out research and teaching whilst continuing to treat patients; professors of education rarely teach in schools, even when their research is school-focused, and school teachers are rarely involved in research. Perhaps partly as a direct consequence of this, the link between teaching in schools and education research is weak.

There are some hopeful straws in the wind suggesting that the relationship between school teaching and research will become closer, however. Teachers have increasing opportunities to take part in research projects, such as those sponsored by the EEF, in which more than a quarter of schools in England have taken part, and teaching schools have research as one of their six priority areas, albeit the least well developed of the six.

Alison Wilkinson, head of Queen Elizabeth School, Kirkby Lonsdale in Cumbria has written a blog post on combining headship with doing research for a PhD, in which she concludes:

'Would I recommend doing a PhD to school leaders? Certainly. The trick is never to see the role and the research as separate activities. Everything you learn from academic study comes right back into school and everything you learn doing your day job informs your research. It's very enjoyable to be able to value and use your experience at the same time as challenging yourself to learn in new ways. I can thoroughly recommend it.' [9]

From personal experience of doing a PhD on education while serving as a head, I would agree strongly with these sentiments.

---

9   Alison Wilkinson, 'Attempting the impossible: postgraduate research and school leadership' nctl.blog.gov.uk/2016/01/15/attempting-the-impossible-post-graduate-research-and-school-leadership/

From CPD to JPD

The term CPD is in constant use within the teaching profession, but it is in the creation of opportunities for joint practice development (JPD)[10] with other schools that the best development can occur and bring with it the greatest degree of school improvement. There are many different ways in which JPD can take place – for example, lesson study, action planning, peer reviews, research into a specific shared issue, coaching, or learning walks – but the focus on improving classroom practice through joint working can bring major benefits both to the individual teacher taking part and to the school improvement programme.

In a report on JPD written by senior staff from five teaching school alliances, the National College for Teaching and Leadership (NCTL) states that:

'JPD is not something radically new. It is about making school-based professional development more effective by thinking explicitly about how it is structured and facilitated. But moving from a CPD model to a JPD model is challenging and requires sustained thought and leadership.

JPD was defined by Michael Fielding and colleagues as '...learning new ways of working through mutual engagement that opens up and shares practices with others'. It captures a process that is truly collaborative, not one-way, and the practice is being improved not just moved from one person or place to another.

Traditional approaches to CPD are largely based on transferring knowledge or 'best practices' from an expert presenter to his or her audience. Research shows that this is rarely effective. By contrast, JPD is a process by which individuals, schools or other organisations learn from one another. It has three key characteristics:

- *It involves interaction and mutual development related to practice;*

- *It recognises that each partner in the interaction has something to offer and, as such, is based on the assumption of mutually beneficial learning;*

- *It is research-informed, often involving collaborative enquiry.'* [11]

The challenge for school leaders here is: first, weaning staff away from the view that professional development means attending courses; second, creating

---

10   Professor David Hargreaves has developed the notion of JPD. See, for example, David H Hargreaves, A self-improving school system: towards maturity, National College for School Leadership, 2012, dera.ioe.ac.uk/15804/1/a-self-improving-school-system-towards-maturity.pdf

11   Powerful professional learning: a school leader's guide to joint practice development, National College for Teaching and Leadership, 2016 www.gov.uk/government/publications/powerful-professional-learning-a-school-leaders-guide-to-joint-practice-development

an outward-facing culture in which staff are open to learning from, and with, colleagues in other schools; and third, setting the agenda for JPD activities, which is in line with the development priorities of the schools involved. None of this is easy for school leaders to implement, but the shared benefits make it immensely worthwhile. It is a particularly important process within teaching school alliances, MATs and other groups of schools working in partnership.

Performance management and professional development

In a school with an embedded learning culture, CPD is not an occasional foray but an entitlement for every member of the teaching and support staff. For most staff, I took the view as a school leader that performance management should be 20 per cent judgemental and 80 per cent developmental, so that the whole performance management process is set within a context of development. Performance management discussions soon move from 'How am I doing?' to 'What learning opportunities are there to take me to the next stage of improvement?'

It is never easy to deal with staff who are under-performing, but the responsibility cannot be avoided if the school is to be successful. For these teachers, the judgement/development balance may be different, and the development opportunities more urgent and more strongly directed, but the process is still set within a developmental context.

In my work as national pupil premium champion, I spent a good deal of time talking with school leaders about the role and performance of teaching assistants. The deployment and impact of support staff (DISS) project[12] unearthed some alarming data on the way in which teaching assistants were used in the classroom. For example, a high proportion of teaching assistants interviewed said they frequently entered the classroom not knowing what was about to happen in the lesson, and then being utilised in ways that made a small group of children over-dependent on them. Following the DISS report, the EEF published a seven-point guide to the effective use of teaching assistants and a team from the UCL Institute of Education, led by Rob Webster, produced an excellent book on the subject.[13]

---

12 Peter Blatchford et al, The deployment and impact of support staff, DfES, 2009
    www.oxfordprimary.co.uk
    fdslive.oup.com/www.oup.com/oxed/primary/literacy/osi_teaching_assistants_
    report_web.pdf?region=uk

13 Jonathan Sharples et al, Making best use of teaching assistants, Education
    Endowment Foundation, 2015 educationendowmentfoundation.org.uk/uploads/
    pdf/TA_Guidance_Report_Interactive.pdf and Rob Webster et al, Maximising
    the Impact of Teaching Assistants: Guidance for school leaders and teachers,
    Routledge, 2015

While one inevitably concludes from this research that teaching assistants need better training, it is probably even more essential that teachers are well trained in the most effective use of teaching assistants, and that school leaders and governing boards look again at their policies on the deployment of teaching assistants, taking into account the DISS research and the publications that followed it.

Performance management systems for support staff are often weaker than those for teachers, with the consequence that there is a lower level of expectation about the quality of their work. School leaders should evaluate the performance management for support staff and ask themselves the questions, 'How much positive impact is each member of the support staff having and how do we know how effective s/he is?' Equally vital, if challenging, is to ensure that the quantity and quality of professional development opportunities available to support staff are as great as that for teachers.

Professional development standards

For the first time, an expert group of teachers, chaired by David Weston of the Teacher Development Trust, has set out standards for effective professional development.[14] The standards state that teacher professional development should be a partnership between school leaders, teachers and professional development providers, with a focus on improving and evaluating pupil outcomes, robust evidence, collaboration and expert challenge, and sustainability over time. The standards emphasise the importance of leaders prioritising professional development in each school, which is the over-arching message of this chapter.

Following an independent review by a group of school leaders, chaired by Dame Dana Ross-Wawrzynski, executive headteacher of Altrincham Grammar School for Girls and CEO of the Bright Futures Educational Trust, with Roy Blatchford, director of the National Education Trust as vice-chair, headteacher standards were updated in 2015.[15] Their report identified 24 characteristics expected of an excellent school leader, split into four domains: qualities and knowledge, pupils and staff, systems and process, and the contribution that heads make to the self-improving school system.

---

14 Standard for teachers' professional development, Department for Education, 2016 www.gov.uk/government/publications/standard-for-teachers-professional-development

15 Department for Education, National standards of excellence for headteachers: Departmental advice for headteachers, governing boards and aspiring headteachers, HMSO, 2015. See also Roy Blatchford, A Practical Guide: National Standards of Excellence for Headteachers, John Catt, 2015

Enhancing the teaching profession

Since 1988, teachers have gradually been de-professionalised by the government's detailed centralist policies, especially on assessment, and there is no sign of any willingness on the part of the government to change this situation. Other professions, such as medicine and law, would not have stood for it, but teachers have meekly accepted it and, in many cases, come back for more guidance and direction, such has been the lack of self-confidence in the teaching profession.

During his brief spell as shadow secretary of state for education, Tristram Hunt proposed in 2014 that there should be a version of the Hippocratic Oath for teachers. There are many versions of the Hippocratic Oath, and it is not compulsory for doctors in the UK to sign it, although some medical schools have an oath-swearing ceremony. The General Medical Council (GMC) has 'Good Medical Practice' standards, which are the equivalent of the Hippocratic Oath, setting out core values and principles in four domains: knowledge, skills and performance; safety and quality; communication, partnership and teamwork; and maintaining trust.

A successful GTC would have given this kind of principled leadership to the teaching profession, but it did not have the full support of teachers or some of their unions. Having come into being after over 100 years of campaigning for a GTC in England, it lasted only 12 years and was abolished, largely unlamented, by Michael Gove in 2012. This occurred in the aftermath of a particularly weak judgement on the case of a teacher who was a member of the British National Party and wrote extreme racist comments. The loss of the GTC was a seriously wasted opportunity on the part of teachers and their representative bodies in England.

The GTC in Scotland was founded in 1965 and has a strong place in the Scottish education system 50 years later. It is no coincidence that teaching is more strongly placed as a profession in Scotland than it is in England.

The medical profession has its Royal Colleges and, following the failure of the GTC in England, it is welcome that there are plans to establish a College of Teaching. If given some financial support by the government and a strong indication from ministers that they would stop trespassing on professional territory and leave significant matters to the College, this profession-led initiative will make a valuable contribution to teaching as a profession. With an established College, we can more strongly hope that education ministers will no more think of telling teachers how to teach than health ministers would want to tell surgeons how to take out an appendix.

Leadership development

Opened in 2000 by Tony Blair, the National College for School Leadership (NCSL), with Steve Munby as its chief executive from 2005, had become a world-class institution. On the rare occasions when, as ASCL general secretary, I attended international conferences for school principals, it was clear to me how highly the College was regarded across the education world.

In my meetings with Michael Gove before the 2010 general election, I repeatedly told him how important the College was in a policy climate where more responsibility and accountability were being placed on school leaders. I said to him that however many quangos he shut down, he must not close the College, nor must he merge it with the TDA, which had a very different purpose and culture from the College. It was essential that the College should remain independent of the DfE, so that school leaders continued to feel ownership of the College and commitment to its high standards. '*Your government is not going to close Sandhurst, so don't close the College*', was my advice to him. This he spectacularly ignored by merging NCSL and the TDA to form the National College for Teaching and Leadership (NCTL), bringing it into the Department as an executive agency of the government, and appointing a weak chief executive to replace the excellent Steve Munby. All except one of the College's senior staff left within a year.

The College's governing council, on which I sat for its last three years, had a broad membership from education and business, and provided a good sounding board and accountability mechanism for the CEO and the College's executives; now the senior College staff are directly responsible to ministers and civil servants in the DfE. Whereas the College was a focal point for leadership development and forward thinking, NCTL is rarely mentioned by school leaders. It does some good work, but it is viewed by school leaders simply as part of the Department, with strategic thinking and training in leadership development now taking place elsewhere. The TDA's role in the recruitment of teachers has been downgraded, with major consequences for the school system.

The involvement of school leaders in the NCSL meant that the organisation was both owned and led by the leaders of the profession. Many of the most outstanding headteachers in England were regular contributors to college seminars and courses, and had a strong influence on the direction of leadership development in the country. The greatest loss in the move from NCSL to NCTL was the loss of the voice of those leaders at the cutting edge of leadership development thinking and policy at the national level.

Teach First, Future Leaders and Teaching Leaders have done much good work in the field of leadership development and they have a key role to play in producing well-prepared cohorts of leaders for schools – particularly challenging schools – in the future, but their task has been made harder by the government's undermining of the National College.

A new professional development landscape?

A unique opportunity is emerging in 2016 for school leaders and teachers to re-configure the landscape of professional development.

The sad demise of the National College has created a vacuum for leadership development into which ASCL, the NAHT and the National Governors Association (NGA) have stepped to form the Foundation for Leadership in Education, an independent, profession-led body which is well placed to take on the mantle of the college. With Sir Michael Barber, chief education adviser at Pearson and former head of the prime minister's delivery unit, as chair, and Stephen Munday, executive principal of Comberton Village College in Cambridgeshire, as vice-chair, it is envisaged that the Foundation will plan clear progression routes for school leader development and will quality-assure other organisations providing leadership training. The Foundation will have a board of trustees and its work will be developed in consultation with the profession.

Separately from this, a group of senior staff from teaching schools and academy chains is building a partnership to establish a new higher education institute to develop expert teachers for challenging schools. This group has emerged following a report from the Institute for Public Policy Research (IPPR)[16], which proposed that the profession should take the lead in setting up an Institute for Advanced Teaching (IAT) as an independent social enterprise to train qualified teachers with high potential to work in challenging schools on a specially designed master's degree. The IPPR work was sponsored by Ark Schools, Oasis Community Learning, Dixons Academies in the Bradford area, Mossley Hollins High School in Greater Manchester, and two schools mentioned in earlier chapters, Lampton School in Hounslow and School 21 in Newham, whose leaders are taking forward the planning of the Institute. Plans for the academy are set out in figure 9 below.

---

16   Matthew Hood, Beyond the plateau: the case for an Institute for Advanced Teaching, IPPR, 2016 www.ippr.org/publications/beyond-the-plateau-the-case-for-an-institute-for-advanced-teaching

The IAT's three-step plan
A flow-chart of the Institute for Advanced Teaching's objectives, and how they will be achieved

1. Recruit high-potential, qualified teachers who work in challenging schools.	**Associates** • High-potential, qualified teachers who work in challenging schools • Recruited through a rigorous process that assesses their knowledge, craft and values.
2. Develop them into highly expert teachers.	**Master's in advanced teaching** • Two-year part-time master's qualification completed alongside full-time employment. • Accreditation through an existing university in the interim; in the longer term, accreditation by the IAT itself. • Taught by a faculty of the UK's most expert practicing teachers, known as 'fellows'. • Campuses co-located within high-performing schools that serve low-income communities.
3. Build them into a movement for change in education.	**Alumni** • After graduation, alumni are supported to lead improvements in teacher development in their schools, to support new associates and, in some cases, to join the IAT faculty as a fellow.

Figure 9 Plans for the Institute for Advanced Teaching, IPPR, 2016

The CIEA, described in chapter 4, is also a profession-led body providing high-level qualifications to experts in the field, both for those working in schools and colleges and those who work for awarding bodies.

There is surely much to be gained through these three bodies working in partnership to provide a coherent range of qualifications for expert teachers and school leaders, perhaps under the aegis of the College of Teaching. Much more than in the past, the opportunity is there for school leaders to take responsibility for advanced professional and leadership development and create a profession-led suite of development opportunities that would play a part in system-wide school improvement.

***

There are many ways in which school leaders can 'water the plants' for whom they are responsible. There are few things more significant in school leadership than creating a learning climate for staff and providing in-depth opportunities for them to develop professionally and engage with research. Especially in the field of professional development, no school is an island: encouraging staff to look outwards to evidence and to excellent practice in other schools is a vital component of school leadership.

Teaching school alliances and MATs have a role to play as vehicles for partnership working and joint practice development. The leaders of schools in alliances and trusts are instrumental in creating the wider professional development community at all levels from initial training to executive headship, with a special responsibility to identify and develop the leaders of the future.

The teaching profession has suffered some significant blows and negative publicity in the last 30 years, some externally imposed and some self-inflicted. Making teaching into a stronger, more evidence-informed, more outward-looking profession, upholding profession-led standards and taking greater responsibility for professional decisions, such as external assessment grades, is an important part of the wider role of school leadership.

It serves no useful purpose to lead a chorus of complaint about government interference and over-accountability, unless leaders of the profession are prepared to be more evidence-informed, more innovative and take greater ownership of accountability, as discussed in chapter 5. Leading a reconfiguration of the professional development landscape, which has made a good start with the profession-led standards and the plans for a Foundation for Leadership in Education and an Institute for Advanced Teaching, demonstrate that there is an appetite to do things differently in the future. Learning leaders will be at the heart of this work.

Chapter 8

School leadership

*If your actions inspire others to dream more, learn more,
do more and become more, you are a leader.*
John Quincy Adams

The starting-point for this book was the 'ten things learned on my leadership journey' and several of these have been explored in the first seven chapters: values-based leadership; opportunities to be innovative; the prime focus of leadership being on teaching, learning and assessment; the need to look outwards, not upwards, and to encourage staff to do this in their own professional development; and opportunities that come to school leaders to 'water the plants'.

All of this has been set in the historical context I have directly experienced since joining a school leadership team in 1974. School leadership has changed in many ways over these years – and so it should: it would be a sad indictment if it had stayed the same.

I reflected on these changes in a blog post in September 2012[1] on the thirtieth anniversary of becoming a head. While curriculum autonomy has decreased, autonomy in management and financial decisions has grown considerably. Accountability has massively increased from infrequent inspections and unpublished results to regular inspections and a range of published accountability measures. Governing boards that were almost powerless have had their responsibilities increased exponentially.

---

1   johndunfordconsulting.co.uk/2012/09/08/then-and-now-30-years-of-education-policy/

The budget over which a 1200-pupil school had control in 1982 was around £30,000; a school of comparable size now has a budget of several million pounds. In the 1980s, the local authority decided on the number of staff in each school and how many could be at each grade from deputy head down to responsibility allowance A. The local authority also decided how many support staff a school could have, and what roles they could be given.

During the falling rolls of the 1980s, the local authority operated a system of staff redeployment from unfilled schools to more popular schools, preventing successful schools advertising for staff and redeploying many square pegs into round holes. The greatest benefit for heads and governing bodies in the introduction of LMS in 1990 was not the control over more money, but the ability to be able to appoint staff and decide the staffing structure, both for teaching and support. LMS proved to be a watershed in school autonomy, being viewed as central to the agenda of school improvement.

My period of headship, from 1982 to 1998, was divided in half by the introduction of LMS, and there was never any doubt in my mind as to which half I enjoyed more. School leaders in the 21st century may have become more accountable and vulnerable, with far greater responsibility, but the job has become much more fulfilling, with achievement hugely improved, the curriculum out of the secret garden that James Callaghan described in his Ruskin College speech of 1976, assessment for learning to complement assessment of learning, more data to enable policies to be better targeted, and more reliable and accessible evidence on which to draw to raise attainment and close the gaps.

Trends in school leadership

During this period, it is possible to discern several trends in school leadership policy and practice – from head-centric leadership to more distributed leadership, from leadership focused almost entirely on a single school to co-leadership of the school system, with increased powers for heads and governing bodies, and a policy climate changing between collaborative and competitive, centralisation and decentralisation.[2]

However, these trends cannot be represented by neat straight lines. Certainly, the role of the head has become less autocratic and responsibilities have steadily become more distributed. The managerialism of the 1990s, when heads often took a detailed interest in school finances in the early stages of LMS, has given

---

2   See the table of leadership phases in Robert Hill, Achieving more together, ASCL, 2008, which drew on a paper for the Australian Centre for Strategic Education: John Dunford, School leadership: the challenges being faced by English secondary schools, CSE seminar series no. 168, 2007.

way to a broader leadership role. The range of people on the school leadership team has widened and now includes one or more school business leaders who have distinct and important roles. This increase in breadth has been matched by an increase in accountability, with headteachers becoming more vulnerable as a consequence.

Up to the mid-1980s, there was collaboration between schools, but it was more of a tacit agreement not to compete than positive partnership working for the common good. During the Conservative government of the 1980s and the first two-thirds of the 1990s, education policies created a culture of competition between schools, with greater parental choice and open enrolment encouraging schools to replace the turgid typed prospectuses common in many local authority areas with glossy publications. Accountability and parental choice were boosted by the publication of inspection reports and test and examination results. A clear divide appeared between grant-maintained schools and those deciding to remain with the local authority, with considerable competition and tensions emerging between schools in many parts of England.

Since 1997, the matrix of collaboration and competition has created a more complex picture. During the early years of the New Labour government, accountability intensified through the 'naming and shaming' by Labour ministers, just 18 days into office in 1997, of the 'worst' state schools. There was a cap on the number of specialist schools at first, so schools competed for the status and additional funding. Many other funding pots were subject to competitive bidding. However, the New Labour era also saw the evolution of specialist schools into a more partnership-based programme and initiatives such as the London Challenge and the introduction of national leaders of education (NLEs) established the practice of school-to-school support.

2003 saw the opening of the first city academy. The academies programme illustrates both the drive towards strong autonomy for schools but also, as the academy movement has evolved to comprise mainly multi-academy trusts, it has demonstrated the value of schools supporting each other.

The coalition government in 2010 intensified this dual approach. The introduction of free schools, the opening up of academy status to all 'good' schools and more extensive accountability measures published in league table form reinforced competitive pressures. At the same time, the government espoused the concept of moving towards a self-improving school-led system. The creation of a network of teaching schools, enabling schools to play more of a role in recruiting and training teachers through School Direct and the funding of the EEF encouraged more systematic collaboration between schools. Since 2015 the emphasis has moved from softer or more informal partnerships to formal trusts that have a much stronger focus on accountability for school improvement.

The tension between competition and collaboration is nowhere more apparent than in school admissions. In the 1980s and for much of the 1990s the local authority, with the exception of faith schools, set and operated school admissions. However, as academies have control of admissions and with two-thirds of secondary schools designated as academies, admissions are now much more fragmented. Secondary schools tend to compete sharply for year 7 pupils and protocols and arrangements to accommodate vulnerable pupils are under strain in some areas.

The tensions for school leaders caused by having government policies that promote both competition and collaboration are matched by tensions between centralisation and decentralisation. This dichotomy emerged in the late 1980s, when the rhetoric of government ministers emphasised the decentralisation of power through LMS and grant-maintained schools, while the national curriculum, national tests and national inspections of individual schools greatly increased the government's central control of the work of schools.

Similarly, a trend has been evident of increased power and influence for headteachers beyond their own schools through the leadership of multi-academy trusts and teaching schools, executive headship, increased involvement – and that of some of their colleagues – in school-to-school support, initial teacher training and professional development. This has given school leaders an unprecedented opportunity to lead the system, as we shall see in chapter 9.

Yet, even as leaders of academies, heads experience the tensions caused by the DfE exercising direct power over their schools through funding agreements, with regional schools commissioners acting on behalf of the Department. Taken together with the sheer volume of education acts, regulations, initiatives and policy announcements, bringing frequent changes to curriculum, tests and examinations, school structures, accountability measures and funding, many heads feel that there is more central control than ever.

Toby Greany analysed this situation well in his inaugural lecture at the Institute of Education, London.[3] In a blog post in March 2014, he identified the criteria for a self-improving school system and set out four policy approaches that the government is following simultaneously, describing the consequent tensions:

3   Toby Greany, The self-improving school system: competing policies undermine the coalition's admirable aims, Institute of Education blog, 6 March 2014, and Self-improving school system: will it be survival of the fittest or team effort?, Institute of Education blog, 20 March 2014, ioelondonblog.wordpress.com/2014/03/20/self-improving-school-system-will-it-be-survival-of-the-fittest-or-team-effort/

In the *world class (no excuses) approach*, the government is raising the bar in every area and benchmarking England against the best in the world, introducing a new curriculum, more rigorous exams and less teacher assessment. Ofsted inspections are rigorous and, where a school is found to be failing, a new academy sponsor will be found.

In the *freedom to teach approach*, the government gives schools maximum autonomy and focuses accountability on what matters: the quality of teaching. The government claims to have increased freedom over classroom discipline, the removal of much bureaucratic guidance, the removal of the requirement for teachers in academies to have qualified teacher status, the introduction of regulations making it easier to sack poor teachers and pay good teachers more. Schools have been given a greater role in teacher training.

In the *market-based approach*, the government has abolished quangos and cut the number of DfE civil servants. The government would argue that it has encouraged schools to become academies and thus free from LA interference, with more free schools, university technical colleges and studio schools, creating greater competition between schools, challenging weak schools to improve and giving parents greater choice.

In the *system leadership approach*, the government wants the best schools and heads to lead improvement. Over 400 academy sponsors and 600 teaching schools are leading the way on this, with 1000 NLEs designated to improve schools needing support.

This confusion of policies creates a complex environment for school leaders, which requires a very strong moral compass and a wide range of skills and behaviours to enable them to keep their schools on a steady and successful course. The opportunities for school leaders to change the lives of young people beneficially have never been greater, but the policy climate in which they work has never been more confusing.

An optimistic view of school leadership is not easy to sustain day in and day out, but that is exactly what the best school leaders do. With relentless optimism, they make the most of every opportunity available to them.

They focus on what is important and on what will make the greatest positive difference. Sir Tim Brighouse, who has been a constant source of inspiration to me and to thousands of teachers and school leaders, has listed the 'six tasks of school leadership':[4]

- Create energy
- Build capacity
- Meet and minimise crisis
- Secure and enhance the environment
- Seek and chart improvement
- Extend the vision of what's possible.

These chime with the theme of this book, in which creating energy and building capacity have been viewed as particularly important.

Successful school leadership: twelve leadership behaviours

Both during headship and since then in the various roles that I have counted myself privileged to have held, coming into contact with many of the best school leaders in the UK, I have observed a set of behaviours common to successful headteachers and other school leaders.

Among these people, who have chosen to use their many talents in school leadership, but would have been successful in whatever career they had chosen, their leadership is:

- principled
- authentic
- adaptable
- learning-focused
- distributed
- servant
- outward-looking
- creative
- restless
- resilient
- communicative
- optimistic

---

4   Tim Brighouse, How successful head teachers survive and thrive, RM, 2010, support.rm.com/_rmvirtual/Media/Downloads/How_head_teachers_survive_and_thrive_by_prof_Tim_Brighouse.pdf

Not all good school leaders put all of these behaviours into practice on a daily basis, but these are the leadership characteristics needed for schools to be great places of learning in the 21st century.

Principled leadership

We live in an era where political discourse is frequently based on misleading information or untruths. This is not a new phenomenon. The basis for the invasion of Iraq is the most obvious recent example, but there have been plenty of others. Economic debate during the 2015 general election was based around the Conservatives' promise to remove the UK's budget deficit in five years, which they must have known to be impossible. In the EU referendum campaign, the Leave side's case centred around the slogan on its campaign bus that the £350 million pounds a week that the UK pays into the EU could be saved and used for the National Health Service, a calumny that was repeated by Boris Johnson, Michael Gove and leading Leave campaigners even after it had been shown to be false. As soon as the Conservatives had won the election and the Leave campaign had triumphed in the referendum, those who had made the claims stepped back from them.

In the summer of 2016, the new government of Theresa May put out the falsehood that the number of grammar schools should be increased in order to improve social mobility, when the evidence points inexorably to grammar schools being socially selective.

It is in this climate of political deviousness that the first characteristic of successful school leaders should be principled leadership, given the responsibilities they have towards the young. The core message of this book has been that leadership has to be values-based, applying a strong moral purpose and a consistent set of principles to the way in which the school is led. The main task within that is to bring together a group of individuals with different experiences and qualifications into a coherent, collaborative team that works for the good of the learners. High-performing teams flourish under principled leadership.

The American academic, Victor Lopez, has set out ten characteristics of principled leaders in business, government and the academic world:[5]

1. *'They put the interests of the institution they serve above their own self-interest.*

---

5   Victor D Lopez, Ten common characteristics of principled leaders, 2011 blog at tencharacteristicsofprincipledleaders.blogspot.co.uk/2011/08/principled-leadership-in-academia_26.html

2. *They understand that character is defined by the small acts they perform when nobody is looking.*

3. *They recognize that respect must be earned over time but can be lost in an instant.*

4. *They promote their people, not themselves.*

5. *They take responsibility for failure – by themselves and by others.*

6. *They share credit for their successes with the individuals who made them possible.*

7. *They are consistent and predictable in their decision-making.*

8. *They strive to do what is right rather than what is expedient.*

9. *They do not fear making unpopular decisions and clearly communicate their rationale for making such decisions to those affected by them.*

10. *They only serve institutions that do not require them to compromise their principles.'*

Although written mainly from the business perspective, these characteristics fit well with the principled leadership of schools in the 21st century.

Principled leadership promotes clarity among staff, learners, parents and the community, engaging everyone connected to the school in its vision of a high-quality education. Improvement becomes more sustainable. Messages become more consistent. If parents have an issue to raise with the school, it will not matter whether they discuss it with the head or with another member of staff; the way in which the school deals with the concern will be the same.

Authentic leadership

'Achieving business results over a sustained period of time is the ultimate mark of authentic leadership. It may be possible to drive short-term outcomes without being authentic, but authentic leadership is the only way to create long-term results.' [6]

The leaders of the schools featured in the Ofsted series of papers on outstanding secondary, primary and special schools[7] were almost all long-standing heads who built excellence over time. Working in challenging areas, as all of these

---

6   Bill George, Peter Sims, Andrew N. McLean, Diana Mayer, 'Discovering Your Authentic Leadership', Harvard Business Review, February 2007

7   Twelve outstanding secondary schools: excelling against the odds, Ofsted, 2009; Twenty outstanding primary schools: excelling against the odds, Ofsted, 2009; Twelve outstanding special schools: excelling through inclusion, Ofsted, 2009

schools are, it is possible to lead a quick turnaround, but there are many other examples of such schools falling back afterwards. Truly outstanding schools, such as those identified by Ofsted in these papers, grow their success more slowly and consistently, with the headteacher building a broad leadership team and committed staff around a clear set of values.

All the heads of these schools demonstrated authentic leadership. They are reflective people, who are both aware of the challenges they face and self-aware in ways that give them an inner confidence about what they are doing.

Morpeth School in Tower Hamlets featured in both *Twelve outstanding secondary schools* and in Alison Peacock's *Assessment for Learning without limits*.[8] Ofsted noted that, under the steady leadership of Sir Alasdair MacDonald, '*staff are trusted and valued, expectations are high and the school is deeply embedded in the life of the area it serves. … The powerful culture and ethos is based on a strong, shared commitment to meeting children's often complex needs. … This strong sense of commitment begins with the headteacher. When asked about his strengths, staff frequently cite 'moral purpose', 'integrity' and 'trust'. The emphasis is on developing and sustaining the right climate and then trusting staff to do the right thing.*' The report commented on Alasdair's reflective approach and concluded, '*Everyone knows what the school's priorities are.*' Alison Peacock also commented on the trust and consistency at the centre of the leadership of the school.

In the schools mentioned in the three Ofsted publications and in those cited in Alison Peacock's book, the leaders modelled the behaviour for the whole staff. Their authentic leadership was recognised by their colleagues on a daily basis.

Authentic leaders seek feedback on their performance and that of the school, and this promotes openness in the way the school operates. They deal honestly with other people and value their input – and the people know that their words are valued.

Early in his book, *Leadership matters*,[9] Andy Buck stressed the importance of self-awareness and regular review of one's own performance – making the time to reflect, asking for feedback and having a critical friend.

As a head for 16 years and general secretary of ASCL for 12 years, I was in for the long haul in both jobs. Cultural change was a priority in both organisations and I knew that I could not pretend to be what I was not in order to try to achieve change more quickly. I learned that calm, authentic, authoritative, but

---

8   Peacock, op.cit., 2016, p.124
9   Andy Buck, op.cit., 2016

not authoritarian, leadership was what was needed; that there were no magic bullets or instant solutions; that staff would accept culture change, but not all at the same speed.

With authentic leadership comes humility, the recognition of one's own limitations and faults, and the acknowledgement that the success of a school results from the efforts of teams of people. In *Good to great*, Jim Collins describes a Level 5 leader as *'building enduring greatness through a paradoxical blend of personal humility and professional will'*.[10] Andy Buck picked up this point and wrote about the power of humility.[11] I have never met a truly outstanding leader in any walk of life who did not have a high degree of humility.

In contrast to this, I have edited many articles and chapters of books written by I-specialists. These are the heads who write about their school in the first person – 'I am a language college' – and who attribute the success of their schools to themselves, tracing the school's journey from the day they arrived to the excellent test or examination results the school has just achieved. They are often to be heard at conferences, spending half their allotted time talking about 'the context of the school' and claiming credit for all its improvements. This is the antithesis of authentic leadership and is unlikely to bring about sustainable change.

Adaptable leadership

In an Ofsted inspection of Durham Johnston Comprehensive School in 1994, the inspector assigned to evaluate leadership and management had no school leadership experience himself. Interviewing me, he asked about my leadership style. I suggested to him that I was the wrong person to ask and he should find out about my leadership style from other people in the school.

Afterwards I reflected on this conversation, without ever being able to identify one particular style in my leadership of the school. I subsequently realised that leaders do not, and should not, have a single style, but adapt their leadership to the situation. The style adopted when the fire alarm goes off is very different from the way one operates when planning a new behaviour policy for the school. Leadership style must suit the context.

It was therefore disappointing to hear the chief inspector, Sir Michael Wilshaw, in 2011 call for more heads to be like Clint Eastwood, conjuring an image of the headteacher riding into school in front of his staff, shooting enemies and telling everyone to follow him. School leadership may have felt like that to

---

10   Jim Collins, Good to great, Random House, 2001, p.20

11   Andy Buck, op.cit., p.44

Michael Wilshaw when he took on the immense task of building Mossbourne Academy from the ashes of Hackney Downs School in East London, but that is a particular context well outside the daily experience of most school leaders. Michael admitted in a speech five years later that Clint was not always the right model for school leaders. In praising maverick leaders, he said:[12]

'What I neglected to say was that Clint is not suitable for every eventuality. What my mavericks taught me was that great teachers and heads weigh up their students and schools very quickly and adapt their teaching and leadership style to suit.

A maverick leader adapts. They refine their act. They appreciate, for instance, that what may work with unresponsive children won't cut the mustard with implacable staff. The unconventional can be very effective. But even Clint, when the occasion demanded, swapped a rifle for a guitar.'

The great conductor, Sir Colin Davis, who died in 2013, was far from the self-aggrandising maestro that is the image of many famous conductors. According to those who wrote about him after his death, he had humility, integrity and generosity. He could be demonstrative in his conducting, but when I saw him conduct an opera he barely moved his arms, conducting with affirmative nods at critical points. He knew that the orchestra knew what to do and he let them do it.

In politics, leaders are lauded for their 'strong' leadership, but, as in orchestral conducting, this is often not the way to success. In his book *The myth of the strong leader,* Professor Archie Brown shows that the political leaders who made the most sustainable difference to their countries and to the world – transformational leaders such as Nelson Mandela, Deng Xiaoping, Mikhail Gorbachev, Adolfo Suarez and Charles De Gaulle – did not lead their countries in ways that would traditionally have been described as 'strong'.[13] In each case, and that of other political leaders cited in the book, their leadership style suited the circumstances in which they found themselves.

Leading an outstanding school, not losing the good aspects during periods of change; leading a school that is giving a poor standard of education; taking on the leadership of a complacent school that is 'coasting', to use the government's terminology; leading a school that appears to have excellent examination results, but where the poor performance of disadvantaged learners has been

---

12   www.gov.uk/government/speeches/sir-michael-wilshaws-speech-to-the-tes-leadership-conference

13   Archie Brown, The myth of the strong leader: political leadership in the modern age, Vintage Books, 2015

hidden behind the headline achievements of their more fortunate peers; leading a school at times of funding cutbacks; leading a school in a partnership or multi-academy trust – all these situations demand different styles of leadership. As Andy Buck stated, *'understanding your context is crucial before deciding upon priorities for action and approach to implementation.'* [14]

Learning-focused leadership

Leading teaching is the most important aspect of being a school leader. In chapter 7, the leadership of professional development for staff centred on the notion of the learning school and it is through the leadership of this that school leaders can bring the greatest influence to bear on the quality of education of the younger learners.

In a book on passionate leadership, John Macbeath stated that the distinguishing mark of passionate leaders is that they breathe life and excitement into their schools and he quoted Sackney and Mitchell:[15]

'We have found that, in successful schools, learning leaders know the people, the organisations, the communities and the contexts; they ask questions rather than provide answers; and they know what is happening with teaching and learning. Most importantly, they find ways to release the creative energies of teachers and students, for this is the force that fosters experimentation and that breathes life, excitement and enthusiasm into the learning environment for students and for teachers. This implies, of course, that the leaders are comfortable with ambiguity and that they trust teachers and students to work their magic in the classrooms.'

This element of trust, backed up by encouragement, is at the centre of the learning culture set out by Alison Peacock in the notion of *learning without limits*. In her book, she mentioned seven key dispositions that underpin leadership and teaching and enabled her school to improve from the difficult position in which it had been:

- *'Openness to ideas*
- *Questioning, restlessness and humility*
- *Inventiveness allowing for creativity*
- *Persistence and professional courage*

---

14 Andy Buck, op.cit. p.55

15 John Macbeath, 'Not so much a passion, more a way of life', in Brent Davies and Tim Brighouse (eds.), Passionate leadership in education, Sage, 2008, p.124 The quote is from L. Sackney and C. Mitchell, 'Leadership for learning: a Canadian perspective', in John Macbeath and Y.C. Chen, Leadership for learning: international perspectives, Sense Publishers, 2007.

- *Emotional stability enabling risk-taking*
- *Generosity that welcomes difference and diversity*
- *Empathy offering mutual supportiveness.*

If we trust that colleagues want to do their best, we are placed in a leadership position that can afford to be open, creative and empathic. It feels enabling to lead from a position of ambitious optimism with faith in others. Very seldom has this approach let me down.' [16]

As the earlier example of Morpeth School in Tower Hamlets shows, trusted staff who are clear about the values of the school and feel involved in all aspects of its development are willing to take on greater responsibility and accountability for their own work. [17]

Most people come into teaching with some expertise and a passionate desire to teach well and to improve the lives of their pupils. As expertise increases, that passion is sometimes lost, most often because teachers feel they are losing control of their teaching and their professionalism. Re-kindling that passion and stimulating that professionalism are the job of the school leader.

For his chapter in *Passionate leadership in education*, Tim Brighouse interviewed ten headteachers, all of whom agreed that values were at the heart of a passionate and successful school. He quoted one head:

'Why do you think I go to all that trouble? It is because, although we are buffeted by change, there are certain values which act as a moral compass for us all, including me.' [18]

As with so many other facets of leadership, leading learning is a values-based aspect of leadership. Professional development opportunities, empathy, encouragement and trust all play their part in freeing teachers from the constraining feeling that they have to 'deliver' a curriculum that has been handed down to the school from the government using methods approved by Ofsted.

Teaching, learning and assessment of high quality embrace the importance of listening, which can have a big impact on pedagogy and learning. As discussed in chapter 4, listening to the learners and pupils who engage in dialogue about their learning is an essential component of effective teaching. Learning-focused leadership encourages this across the school.

---

16   Alison Peacock, Assessment for learning without limits, Open University Press, 2016, p.6

17   Ibid, p.127

18   Tim Brighouse, 'The passionate teacher and the passionate leader in the passionate school', in Brent Davies and Tim Brighouse, op.cit., 2008, p.28.

Distributed leadership

Ubuntu was the underlying theme of an International Confederation of Principals (ICP) conference in Cape Town in 2005. It is a Bantu principle that has no exactly equivalent meaning in English, but can be roughly translated as 'I am who I am through others'. At the conference, it was a huge privilege to hear Archbishop Desmond Tutu speak about Ubuntu, which is essentially about the inter-connectedness of people and their relationships with others. In school leadership terms, it underscores the importance of distributed leadership, recognising the part played by leaders in different roles at different levels and going beyond the straightforward allocation of responsibilities to a genuinely shared leadership.

Distributed leadership is not confined to a broadly based staffing structure; it is an approach that empowers people in the school beyond the head and senior leadership team to make significant decisions. It stems from the belief that all staff – and learners too – are in leadership roles. As distributed leadership becomes embedded in the staff, people are prepared to take on more responsibility and accountability for their own decisions – this is the flywheel concept described by Jim Collins in *Good to great*.[19] As more staff take on leadership responsibilities, distributed leadership develops a momentum of its own.

As Collins states, though, this does not happen overnight:

'Good-to-great transformations often look like dramatic, revolutionary events to those observing from the outside, but they feel like organic, cumulative processes to people on the inside. ... No matter how dramatic the end result, the good-to-great transformations never happened in one fell swoop. There was no single defining action, no grand program, no one killer innovation, no solitary lucky break, no miracle moment.'

For a new headteacher, distributed leadership starts on day 1. Staff expect the new head to make decisions from the outset, so establishing a culture of distributed leadership with staff taking on greater responsibility may be difficult. As the new head walks along the corridor or into the staff room, s/he is asked questions that invite an immediate decision. Apart from the undesirability of making decisions on the spur of the moment, with the risk that they will be regretted or reversed later, it can be too easy to say yes or no, do this or don't do that. The best response to these questions may not be to show off your shiny new decisiveness, but to suggest that the person herself should decide or that someone other than the head should be asked. Distributed

19   Jim Collins, Good to great, Random House, 2001, p.164

leadership will not come about in reality if the head always feels the need to provide an answer to every question.

The extent of distributed leadership can change over time. As a head and leadership team become more established, the school's values and leadership actions become more embedded. Staff do not feel the need to refer to more senior people because they begin to realise that they can answer their own questions; they take on more responsibility, perhaps without realising it.

If all new policies and practices are decided by the senior leadership team, staff will be less likely to assume responsibility. I had been a head for several years before I realised that every significant new development had been led by a member of the senior leadership team. I also observed that candidates from other schools for senior posts at Durham Johnston tended to have had broader leadership experience if they held middle leadership positions in small secondary schools than if they had been in larger schools where their responsibilities were more compartmentalised.

So, when the senior leadership team decided to establish a staff working party to produce a new homework policy, we invited interested staff to attend and let them decide who should lead the group. Three middle leaders agreed to share the leadership of the group. A good new policy was produced and three middle leaders had whole-school leadership experience. All three subsequently became heads of large secondary schools.

Again, trust comes into the leadership of the school. Building trust takes time and requires a high degree of consistency from the head and senior staff. It depends on leaders respecting staff, whatever their role, and however they see their place in a hierarchy of responsibility posts. Andy Buck draws on the work of Stephen Covey in describing the positive effect of this trust, as leadership is well distributed:[20]

'In teams with a high level of trust, systems and procedures are helpfully aligned and bureaucracy is kept to a minimum. Individuals are trusted and supported to carry out their work. There are positive and transparent relationships amongst staff, leading to innovation, confidence and loyalty. Discretionary effort is high.'

Successful school leaders encourage everyone in the school to exercise leadership, whether they are responsibility postholders, classroom teachers, support staff or students. Distributed leadership can be said to be thoroughly embedded in the school when all these groups and individuals are prepared to take on responsibility and accountability and to be proactive in decision-making.

---

20   Andy Buck, op.cit., p.167. Stephen Covey, The speed of trust: one thing that changes everything, Simon and Schuster, 2008

Student leadership has long had a high priority in the independent sector. Good maintained schools also establish ways in which students are encouraged to take on leadership roles, the context for which may be through school council membership, sport, music, the school library, information technology (in which some students will be well ahead of many of the staff), co-curricular activities and community events. These students are no longer the passive recipients of education but, in line with the values of the school, are assuming leadership roles that will prepare them well for later life. Distributed leadership of this sort becomes part of the school ethos and goes well beyond a standard sharing of staff responsibilities.

Servant leadership

Shortly before he became president of South Africa, Nelson Mandela said:

'I stand here before you filled with deep pride and joy – pride in the ordinary, humble people of this country. I stand before you humbled by your courage, with a heart full of love for you all. I regard it as the highest honour to lead ANC at this moment in our history. I am your servant...'

Steve Munby, then chief executive of the National College for School Leadership, quoted this in 2010 in an influential speech on servant leadership. Instead of saying 'What do I want?' he said, servant leaders ask themselves 'What is wanted of me?' He explained that they lead with moral purpose and see it as their fundamental duty to do everything in their power to act in the interests of those they serve. Their driver, he said, is not to be a leader first and foremost or to seek power as an end in itself; it is to become a leader because they believe that is the best way to make a difference.

Servant leaders, Steve Munby said:

- develop others
- are careful stewards of resources
- understand the context of those they serve and manage change well
- are learners
- collaborate
- are resilient
- hold courageous conversations.

For servant leaders, leadership is not about power or self-importance, but about making a difference by empowering others and supporting them in their leadership roles.

Servant leaders know well the people and the context they serve. They put a high priority on identifying with the needs of the children and the communities in which they work, and on serving them in ways that will lead to improvement. They understand the importance of taking people with them, so have to be good at managing change.

Steve Munby noted that school leaders have to ensure that others can see the outcomes of change clearly and need the leader to be the vision keeper. Staff, learners and the community will support change – even the hardest changes – if they can see that change is conducive to the progress they wish to see. In the words of Peter Senge: *'People don't resist change. They resist being changed.'*

Servant leaders are prepared to work in partnership with other schools and are more likely to hold difficult and courageous conversations, because they regard their leadership role ultimately as one where they serve the children and young people and do whatever is necessary to help them to succeed.

Good leaders both lead and serve their staff. They see success as coming through the efforts of others, so nurture the staff in order to help the school thrive across the full range of its activities. They recognise that, although people rarely say 'well done' or 'thank you' to the head, the head should never lose an opportunity to say it to others.

Support given to others is an essential part of servant leadership – support for staff at every stage of their career; support for teachers in the classroom and in their duties outside; support for staff and parents at parent discussion evenings; support for the governing board in fulfilling its role; support for school sports teams, drama productions and music; creating confidence in the leadership of the school, so staff, learners and parents know that, when something is going wrong, the people at the top will spend time helping them.

Servant leaders act as a sieve of information, legislation and other directives coming into school on an almost weekly basis, only letting through to the staff what they need in order to do their job well. An important leadership tool is the delete button on the computer or the waste paper bin on the office floor, protecting staff from all but the most important information.

Servant leaders value, challenge, support and recognise the achievements of every person in the school.

I once heard an after-dinner speaker say: *'Wherever you are, you can always recognise headteachers. They're the ones picking up the litter.'* The notion of public service may seem old-fashioned to some, but the best school leaders, in embodying servant leadership, believe their job is to be in the service of others. Public service is alive and well on a daily basis in schools.

Outward-looking leadership

There are three reasons why school leaders, and heads in particular, need to be outward-looking. First, school leadership can be a lonely job. Second, schools cannot thrive if they are inward-looking. Third, in being appointed to a school leadership role, one is also taking on the co-leadership of education in the area, with responsibilities to learners well beyond those in one's own school.

When I became a head, there was no national or local scheme of training for the role, no mentoring scheme and I knew no local heads. I was on my own, with only local authority staff to advise me – and the chief adviser was so poor that it was said that, when he left a similar role in a smaller authority to come to County Durham, there had been a leaving party, to which he was not invited.

The local County Durham heads and those who attended the north-east Secondary Heads Association meetings, such as Michael Duffy, the experienced head of King Edward VI School, Morpeth, were my network groups and it was good to have some of them on the end of a telephone when I needed help and support. Nobody should nowadays be expected to take on headship without extensive training and a good mentoring programme in the first few years of the job. Some of the early problems of free schools have come from the absence of training and support for those new to headship. This adds the issues that inevitably arise from opening a new school to the problems often faced by new heads.

Especially within a fragmented school system, school leaders want, and need, to be part of wider education networks, beyond their own school or multi-academy trust. Teaching school alliances partly fulfil this role and many LA-wide leadership groups still exist, but the school leader associations, ASCL and NAHT, have an important part to play in creating social and leadership capital between schools in different parts of the country.

Chains of schools and multi-academy trusts offer a good network of support for new heads and Teach First, Teaching Leaders and Future Leaders all provide first-class networks for their alumni.

The five core beliefs of the excellent Future Leaders programme are: *Every Child, No Excuses, High Expectations, Lead Learning, No Islands.*

No school is an island. Schools exist in the context of their local community and an increasingly national education service. School improvement is taking place more rapidly than ever, both within schools and between schools in groups and trusts. Failure to keep in contact with what is happening nationally and in other schools means that the school will at best stand still, while others are forging ahead. So looking outwards is an essential task for all school leaders, setting an example to all staff to do the same.

An important theme of this book is the opportunity for school leaders to take the initiative and be innovative in every aspect of school life, encouraging staff by example to be creative and not feel overwhelmingly constrained by Ofsted demands and government diktat. Responsible innovation results from learning outside the school what is working well elsewhere, bringing those ideas back into school and adapting them to the school's context. Innovation does not necessarily have to mean inventing new ideas. It can arise from researching evidence of best practice and what is successful in other schools, amending those ideas where necessary and implementing them in the context of the values, policies and practices that are currently working well in one's own school.

After more than a generation of looking up to the government to be told what to do, teachers need active encouragement from school leaders to look outwards to excellent practice – *stop looking up and start looking out* should be the mantra of every school.

An important part of outward-looking leadership is the school's relationship with its partner schools, which will be discussed in the next chapter. Schools can be in many different partnerships and it is part of the role of the school leader to explore potential links that could be of benefit to the learners and staff. With modern communications and the availability of information on the internet, these partnerships can exist well beyond the local area in which the school is situated, allowing school leaders to keep in touch with education developments nationally and internationally.

Creative leadership

As Geoff Barton recalled in chapter 2, Winston Churchill said: '*Headmasters have powers at their disposal with which prime ministers have never yet been invested.*' Allowing for the gender-specific nature of the quote from 1930, the point is nonetheless well made that, even in the confused policy climate of 2016, headteachers have a great deal more decision-making power than leaders in many other jobs.

In spite of the centrally controlled policies mentioned at the start of this chapter, headteachers in England have a high degree of autonomy, compared with school principals in other countries, including Wales and Scotland.

The mixture of autonomy and accountability creates different pressures on school decision-making, according to the position of the school and its leadership. This has produced a situation in which some schools are confident and exercise their autonomy in various ways, while other schools feel constrained by accountability and less able to do anything that might appear to be risk-taking.

Leaders who are clear in their values and who take a broad definition of the curriculum and a proactive approach whenever an opportunity arises have a great deal of space for creativity and innovation, whatever the position of their school.

In chapter 3, three innovations were mentioned which led to interesting projects at Durham Johnston. In each case, an idea occurred to me, which the school was able to put into action, and the breadth of the educational experience of many learners was increased. The artist-in-residence scheme broadened the curriculum for both learners and teachers. It was not difficult to organise and it brought a new perspective into the classroom in art, music, drama and English lessons on a termly basis.

The exchange with Japanese high schools was a life-changing experience for the students who took part. As head of a school, I was in the business of changing young people's lives for the better and maximising the opportunities that were open to them. The Japanese exchange was a good example of both these things, emphasising how school leaders can be proactive in putting their ideas into action in ways that can yield benefits well beyond what was originally imagined.

The third innovation – in public speaking and debating – was discussed in chapter 3 in the context of skills development. This was an example of an idea that achieved far more than I could ever have imagined. In chapter 7, we discussed how the role of headteachers to 'water the plants' could stimulate the school as a learning community for all, enabling staff to grow professionally. Watering the plants applies to pupils too – and one seldom knows how tall and strong the plant will grow. When we discussed the idea of having a junior public speaking competition, we could never have guessed the way in which that particular plant would grow over the following ten years, resulting in Durham Johnston Comprehensive School winning the Observer Mace debating trophy.

When I look back on 16 years of headship, this was my proudest moment. The school's best two debaters, Ian MacMullen and Amanda Pritchard, beat Winchester College and Westminster School, the top debating school from Scotland and many others on their way to being presented by Viscount Hailsham with the silver replica of the parliamentary mace, valued at £45,000 and carried carefully back to Durham on the train in a large wooden box. It was the first time that the word 'comprehensive' had appeared on that august trophy, previously won almost exclusively by independent and selective schools.

The long path to the Observer Mace can be traced from the year 7 and 8 public speaking competition to year 9 students wanting to move from public speaking to debating and two talented teachers, Joan Gibb and Robert Williams, using their knowledge and experience to train generations of debaters, taking the debating teams to competitions all over the country, learning from failures and building on success. As the head, all I had to do was to offer encouragement and a small amount of funding; the plants were growing well.

With the increasing trend for schools to work together, school leaders can now make the sort of opportunities described above available not only to the students in their own school, but in the wider group of schools to which they belong.

Encouraging creativity and innovation means accepting failures as learning experiences, not as reasons for criticism. In Carol Dweck's growth mindset, failure is a learning experience, and this applies as much to school leaders and staff as it does to young people. In the words of Winston Churchill again: *'Success is the ability to move from one failure to another with no loss of enthusiasm.'*

Restless leadership

In the learning-focused leadership discussed above, one of the dispositions mentioned by Alison Peacock as underpinning the leadership required to improve her school so much was 'questioning, restlessness and humility'.

We have to be careful with the definition of 'restless', which can be a negative form of leadership as well as a positive one. If restlessness breeds change for change's sake or introduces changes that are unfocused, it will have a negative effect on the school, which can quickly lose its sense of direction. However, if restless leadership means that the staff are never satisfied with anything less than the best and are constantly on the lookout for what could improve standards, it has a wholly positive effect on the school.

Most school leaders are restless in the early years in a new post, but it takes a special kind of leader still to be restless after ten or more years in the same school and still to have the same drive for improvement. The heads in the three Ofsted publications mentioned above in the section on authentic leadership all served many years in the same school and yet were as restless in the latter part of their headship as they had been at the outset.

As Roy Blatchford – himself a restless leader of schools and of the National Education Trust – has written:[21]

'Successful schools and their leaders are restless. There is a strange paradox at their core: they are very secure in their systems, values and successes, yet

21   Roy Blatchford, The restless school, John Catt, 2014

simultaneously seeking to change and improve. These schools look inwards to secure wise development; they look outwards to seize innovation which they can hew to their own ends and, importantly, make a difference to the children and students they serve.'

Within this thirst for improvement, the staff are focused, because the school leaders are focused and set a clear sense of direction.

Resilient leadership

The capacity to continue to pursue the school's priorities, when external pressures are weighing heavily, is also a feature of resilient leadership. All jobs have setbacks, but jobs that are people-focused, such as teaching and school leadership, are more liable than most to be affected by pressures that are difficult to deal with. Resilient leaders are able to bounce back from these situations and keep the school on a steady course.

This persistence comes from a clear and strongly held set of values, to which resilient leaders return in times of difficulty. It also requires a degree of courage and determination to pursue the same successful outcomes for the school when pressures are seeming to push it in a different direction.

Everything that crops up in school leadership can either be seen as a problem or an opportunity; resilient leaders rebound from problems and use them to create opportunities for their staff and students.

Andy Hargreaves and Dennis Shirley say that two of the key predictors of resilience are a strong sense of purpose and a supportive partnership.[22] The strong sense of moral purpose that drives successful school leaders gives them inbuilt resilience, but the supportive partnership is equally important, as we have seen above, in the need to have outward-looking leadership networks. Because such networks are built over time, some school leaders find they become more resilient with experience.

Communicative leadership

I have often said that good school leadership is 10 per cent action and 90 per cent communication. Whether these proportions are correct is less important than the point that an essential attribute of successful school leadership is to have excellent communication skills. Heads, leadership teams and governing boards can and do make many decisions in a typical week, but none of them will be effective unless communicated well.

---

22   Andy Hargreaves and Dennis Shirley, The fourth way, Corwin Sage Publications, 2009, p.74

Every decision made by the school leadership team during my headship was followed by the team asking itself the questions: 'Who do we tell?' and 'How shall we tell them?'

Communication skills are of three sorts – verbal, written and action-based – and all three may well be needed in order to put a decision into action successfully

The reputation of a school depends not only on the effectiveness of these internal communications, but also on the school's external communications. An essential aspect of school leadership, whether the school is highly successful or on an improvement journey, is telling the wider community about the achievements of the school and its students. No opportunity should be lost to be proactive with external communications.

As discussed in chapter 5, accountability to parents and the community is assuming greater importance, a trend likely to accelerate in a political climate that emphasises the empowerment of citizens in their localities.

The school website is a key communications tool, as are social media, and many schools have become sophisticated in their use of these. It is worth investing in some media training for the head and the senior leader in charge of communications.

Good relationships with the local media can be of great help when a crisis occurs. The journalists will still want their story, but they will be much more willing to report the school's side of the situation and present a balanced picture. In public relations work, school leaders have to be proactive and make the most of any opportunities that arise. There are occasions when marketing can take an unexpected turn. If good relationships have been built with local media, potential positive opportunities are multiplied and the investment of time repaid.

I recall the late August day when a BBC Look North producer telephoned to ask if he could film some clips on the first day of term to mark the new school year and the start of the implementation of yet another new Education Act. The first morning of a new school year tended to be spent sorting out timetables for older students and would have been unlikely to present the school in a good light on regional television. I suggested to the producer that the 'new year, new legislation' theme could best be complemented by filming the year 7 pupils on their first day at Durham Johnston, bright with enthusiasm for their new school and incredibly smart with their new clothing and school bags. A talented teacher, Bernard Clarke, on his first day in the school, found himself being filmed teaching. Those two minutes of publicity on regional television, which had come about through the good relationship the school had built with the BBC over many years, were worth thousands of pounds of more conventional marketing.

At a national level, communication from school leaders is important too. It is an unhappy contrast that, while there are many positive stories about schools in the media, there is the 'constant rhetoric of decline' [23] about the performance of the maintained school system, which is dispiriting for school leaders, teachers, parents and learners. This places an obligation not only on teacher associations, but also on individual school leaders, to maximise positive coverage in local and national media, as a counterweight to the often fact-free articles and editorials denigrating the achievements of state schools and their pupils.

In the 1990s, I recall the usual August curmudgeons being quoted in the media that the improvement in A level results proved that standards must be declining. I arranged for one of the feisty Durham Johnston sixth formers, who had got three A grades, to go on the Today programme immediately before the duty minister from the DfE. To say that he found Grace persuasive is an understatement. '*I know that standards are not falling,*' Grace said, '*we have done lots of past papers and I can tell you that this year it was just as hard to get grade A as in previous years.*' This may not have been a scientific analysis of alleged grade inflation, but the minister could hardly disagree with Grace's articulate account of her A level experience.

The most important communication for school leaders, however, is within the school itself. Being visible is important. Leadership through the soles of your shoes means being around the school at critical times of day – before and after school, breaks, lunchtimes and changes of lesson, for example – and having conversations with students, staff and visitors. When a school leader takes business leaders for a walk around the school, the thing the business people tend to notice, that is most in contrast with their normal working day, is the number of verbal interactions school leaders have with different people during the course of the day. Communicate, communicate, communicate.

Optimistic leadership

Sir Tim Brighouse has been an optimistic leader in his many roles in education. Here he reflects on the qualities needed to be a successful headteacher:

'*I once heard an American say that you needed four things to be a successful head, but it's true of teachers too. You needed unwarranted optimism, you needed to regard crisis and complexity as fun, you needed to have an endless well of intellectual curiosity, so your mind was always racing, even in the middle of things, and finally you needed a complete absence of paranoia and self-pity. And I think*

---

23   Matthew Taylor, Observer, 2 September 2012

those qualities are crucial in teaching, but I think they are absolutely crucial in a head.' [24]

Like all new heads, I started with a combination of apprehension and ambition, but I needed every bit of unwarranted optimism to get me through the first year.

In the 1980s, the local authority managed supply teaching. If a teacher were absent, the school phoned County Hall and they arranged for a supply teacher – an example of the extent of the role of local authorities at that time. To save money, Durham LA decided to stop spending on supply teaching (except for maternity cover) and told school staff that they would have to cover absences themselves. Unsurprisingly, the NASUWT took a dim view of this increase in their members' workload and started a series of strikes, concentrating on three of the schools in the county, one of which was Durham Johnston, where the union's membership was highest. In my first year of headship, therefore, I had to manage the effects of 42 days of strike action, each involving different teachers striking for a different amount of time. This was where the NASUWT honed the action that was to go nationwide in 1984. It was a dark period for me, seeing so much of what I believed about the way in which teachers should work together for the good of the pupils on the bonfire of the local authority's stupidity and the nature of the union's action. It was difficult to be optimistic then, or in 1984, about the future of the profession or of my school in particular.

Every leader has setbacks and this one came very early in my headship, before I had had the chance to establish a new ethos for the school or build any sustainable changes. But it was of no help to dwell on the negatives of this period; if I wanted the school to move forward, I would have to grit my teeth and convey a tone of optimism. All school leaders will have faced similarly discouraging situations at some point.

As noted in chapter 1, it is not possible to communicate positivity with a grim expression and doleful demeanour. Schools should be places of fun and laughter, as well as hard work and opportunity. If the school is to be successful and the staff well motivated, the head has to take the lead in producing an optimistic approach. Smiling is a vital leadership attribute. Problems are there to be overcome, opportunities to be taken and positive encouragement to be given to the learners.

***

---

24   Tim Brighouse, It's the one job I've never had, and always wanted, National
      College for School Leadership, 2010, www.nationalcollege.org.uk/transcript-sp-
      tim-brighouse-.pdf

This chapter has drawn together some of the themes of the preceding seven chapters and put them in the historical context I have experienced during my various leadership roles in education.

The twelve behaviours of successful leaders I have observed in many different school contexts suggest ways in which values-based proactive leadership can make a lasting difference to the lives of the young people in our schools and to the professional experience of the staff who teach them.

While it was good to meet school leaders from other countries at international conferences and to hear about their experiences, my lasting impression was the high regard in which school leadership in the UK is held across the world. Our autonomy and the breadth of our decision-making are widely envied, as are our innovation and creativity. The pastoral support systems and range of extra-curricular activities are admired. School leaders in other countries would love to have the opportunities that we have to work beyond our own school.

An OECD report in 2012 placed UK headteachers at the top of its leadership index for the extent to which their jobs related to the improvement of pedagogy, teaching quality, student progress and curriculum. In the areas of activity that OECD believes make the greatest impact on student success, UK heads are an example to the rest of the developed world.

We have much to learn from school leadership in other countries, but it is good to remember that there are many aspects of leadership in the UK that other education jurisdictions seek to emulate. While government ministers in London frequently introduce changes based on practice overseas, those countries are looking to the UK for the quality of its practice in school leadership.

School leaders have responded positively to the increased opportunities for them to distribute leadership widely across the school and, as will be discussed in the next chapter, to exercise leadership beyond their own school.

Chapter 9

Leading beyond the school

Do all the good you can, by all the means you can, in all the ways you can, in all the places you can, at all the times you can, to all the people you can, as long as ever you can.
John Wesley

The future is already here; it is just not distributed very well.
William Gibson

A new landscape of school leadership

Opportunities for school leaders to work beyond their own school have grown rapidly since about the year 2000 and there is a wide range of roles open to successful leaders at senior and middle level.

It is now accepted that school-to-school support is the most effective and efficient model of improving schools. Central government, in particular, has realised that the greatest expertise in school improvement sits not in local authority offices or in the private sector, but in the schools themselves, although good LAs have retained a co-ordinating role. The success of schemes such as the London Challenge strengthened the resolve of the Labour, coalition and Conservative governments successively to develop this school-led improvement model.

The London Challenge provided lessons for school leaders working in partnership.[1] The greater effectiveness of London schools came through no single magic bullet, but through a combination of factors, a huge amount of hard work and a commitment to the greater good of the schools across the city. Important elements included a critical mass of effective school leadership; successful school leaders working with 'keys to success' schools in other boroughs, which represented positive school-to-school support at its best; relentless focus on the quality of teaching and learning; shared data; improved teacher recruitment, including working with Teach First; a step change in professional development; intelligent, but hard-edged, accountability; and, perhaps of greatest importance, a combination of shared moral purpose, professional challenge and leverage that translated effective support into improved practice.

Central and local government were instrumental in planning and resourcing the London Challenge, but it was the skills and experience of school leaders that provided the expertise to improve the performance of London schools from the worst region in England to the best in a period of ten years. London school leaders have continued their collaborative work through the Good to Great (G2G) and Going for Great (G4G) programmes, under the leadership of Rachel Macfarlane, principal of Isaac Newton Academy, Ilford, and David Woods, the chair of the London Leadership Strategy (LLS). They have edited a series of six case studies of successful London schools, which provide a remarkable catalogue of sustained school-led school improvement, based on 'nine pillars of greatness'.[2]

Much of the current school landscape has evolved from this work in London, with new structures and roles developing locally and nationally. Many school leaders are now working across more than one school in the roles of executive head, leadership of other groups, school-to-school support work, inspection, peer review and committee membership.

The growth of multi-academy trusts

The growth of MATs and teaching schools has been particularly significant in this new landscape. MATs have evolved in a variety of forms, developing many new roles for school leaders and teachers.

There were 21,900 state-funded schools in England in May 2016, of which approximately 5,719 were academies, including 65 per cent of secondary schools

---

1   Sam Baars et al, Lessons from London schools: investigating the success, CfBT, 2014, www.educationdevelopmenttrust.com/en-GB/our-research/our-research-library/2014/r-london-schools-2014

2   Rachel Macfarlane and David Woods (eds.), Unleashing greatness, London Leadership Strategy, 2016. This is the sixth in the series of books published by the LLS since 2010.

and 20 per cent of primaries. There is considerable variation in the pattern of academies across the country, with over 80 per cent of schools in Bournemouth and Bromley being academies, while fewer than 5 per cent are academies in Bury, Lancashire, Lewisham, North Tyneside and St Helens.

There were approximately 2,000 standalone academies and 3,300 schools were in 973 MATs, with half in MATs of four schools or fewer.[3]

Number of MATs by size of MAT

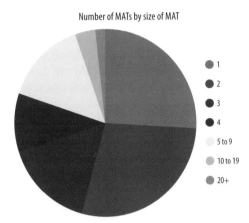

- 1
- 2
- 3
- 4
- 5 to 9
- 10 to 19
- 20+

Figure 10 Number of MATs of different sizes.[4]

Among new MATs in 2016, most are small, with fewer than ten schools, and cross-phase MATs are becoming more common, as are MATs that have a combination of sponsored and convertor academies. More Anglican and Catholic dioceses are forming MATs or participating in the governance of mixed faith and community trusts.

In a series of regional conferences in the summer of 2016, the National Schools Commissioner, Sir David Carter, set out plans for the growth of a school system in which all schools are in MATs, with every school being both a giver and receiver of support, and MATs work together, sharing resources and talent. He recognised that some schools would wish to remain as standalone academies, but hoped that they too would work with other schools.

David Carter envisaged four categories of MAT: starter trusts with 1 to 5 schools and up to 1200 students; established trusts with up to 15 schools and

3   www.gov.uk/government/uploads/system/uploads/attachment_data/file/535604/
    SFR32_2016_text.pdf
4   Jon Andrews, School performance in multi-academy trusts and local authorities 2015, Education Policy Institute, 2016. NB 252 academies have been established as MATs to allow for future expansion.

5000 students; regional trusts with up to 30 schools and 20,000 students; and system trusts with more than 30 schools. The nine RSCs and their headteacher boards agreed the brokering arrangements for new MATs, but David Carter acknowledged the need to increase leadership capacity if his goal is to be met.

Having been a governor of a small primary school in the village where I live in Leicestershire, I was delighted when the opportunity came for the school to become a founding member of a local MAT on 1 September 2016.[5] The local authority had reduced its capacity and so was unable to offer the level of support which the school had been accustomed to receiving in the past. MATs that are rooted in school improvement, professional development and high-quality teaching, learning and assessment are the right way forward for many schools. For small primary schools particularly, or for cross-phase MATs, the opportunities for pupils will be hugely increased.

In my speech to the launch conference of our MAT, I said that the evidence is clear that successful partnership-working between schools in multi-academy trusts is based on nine essential ingredients:

1. Shared values

2. Shared aims

3. A relentless focus on the quality of teaching, learning and assessment – a compelling curriculum, skilful pedagogy and rich assessment

4. A strong belief in the value and potential of every child, no matter what background

5. A deep commitment to professional development across the whole trust

6. Commitment to the success of other schools in the trust as much as to the success of our own school – one for all and all for one

7. Quality assurance. That is, rigorous self-evaluation and peer review of the quality of work in all our schools

8. Sharing data and using it analytically to improve our performance

9. Using resources where they are most needed in the trust

Leadership of the MAT is critical – at senior and middle level, and in the governance structure – to translate these ingredients into policy and practice in each school in the trust.

---

5   This is discussed in more detail in my blog in the Times Educational Supplement at www.tes.com/news/school-news/breaking-views/schools-joining-mats-will-do-better-in-partnership. My speech to the launch conference of the MAT is at johndunfordconsulting.co.uk/blog/

Leading multi-academy trusts

Most MATs are led by executive heads. The exact number of executive heads is not known, but research[6] on the role in 2016 by the National Foundation for Educational Research (NFER), the National Governors' Association (NGA) and the Future Leaders' Trust quoted school workforce data, which found 628 executive heads, working with at least 971 schools. There is no fixed role description for executive headship, not all of whom lead MATs. The roles depend partly on the number of schools in the trust or federation, the strength of the schools and their strategic priorities, and whether the executive head is also the substantive head of one of the schools in the group.

The NFER/NGA/Future Leaders report identified ways in which the role of executive head is different from that of headteacher, with less operational activity, higher levels of strategic thinking, greater emphasis on coaching, delegating and achieving change through others, and more capacity to be outward-looking.

The report also identified professional development needs for executive heads, including leadership and change management theory, managing across school phases, managing human resources and finances in a large business, and building partnerships.

The report called on the DfE to set up a profession-led definition of executive headship to include associated skills, competencies, organisational structures and indicative remuneration, with a variety of operating models.

Wider leadership roles were discussed and promoted at the National College for School Leadership (NCSL) in the 2000s, where the relatively small number of academy chain leaders met regularly with Steve Munby, the NCSL chief executive, to discuss aspects of the role. In 2010, the College produced a report on the role of executive headship,[7] which stated that the number of executive heads had grown from 24 in 2004 to 450 in 2010.

Surveys conducted for the report found that around 90 per cent of executive heads were responsible for two schools, with 95 per cent of the heads being the substantive head of at least one of the schools they were leading, and in 60 per cent of the cases where executive heads were responsible for two schools, they were the substantive head of both schools. 63 per cent of the executive heads were leading primary schools and just under one-quarter were leading secondary schools, with 35 per cent in cross-phase leadership.

6   Lord, P et al, Executive headteachers: what's in a name? A Full Report of the Findings, NFER, NGA and the Future Leaders Trust, 2016

7   Executive heads: summary report, NCSL, 2010 www.gov.uk/government/uploads/system/uploads/attachment_data/file/340000/executive-heads-summary.pdf

Difficulty in recruiting a suitable candidate to be headteacher and the need to improve the performance of a school were the two most commonly cited reasons for the creation of executive head posts; the former reason was more likely to apply to primary schools and the latter to secondary schools.

The report identified several challenges in the executive headship role:

1. The absence of a clear legal framework, including the statutory pay and conditions of service framework

2. A lack of clarity over the role of executive heads in the inspection system

3. Tension between the strategic and operational roles of an executive head

4. Maintaining the confidence of staff and stakeholders, particularly in the early days of executive headship

5. Drifting into a new executive headship model, rather than taking time to choose a governance model that is appropriate to the context and circumstances of the parties involved

6. Underestimating the risks, including the reputational risk, in taking on another school

7. Failing to develop the right relationship with the local authority at a time when the role of local authorities is evolving

Some, but by no means all, of these issues have been addressed since the report appeared.

One of the positive consequences of the growth in executive headship has been the evolution of new routes into headship. A common model is for heads of school to work under executive heads. While these posts include responsibility for every aspect of the operation of a school, they provide leaders with an introduction to headship without the ultimate responsibility that has been a disincentive to many potential heads.

Janet Renou, the RSC in the North of England, put this well:[8]

'For future school leaders, the emerging career ladder offers exciting opportunities around well-defined roles: head of school, headteacher, executive headteacher and now chief executive officer (CEO). These latter roles offer late-career heads an increasing challenge to grow leaders of the future. Developing a head of school by giving them more space and time than can be found in a deputy post allows them to learn the ropes with a focus on teaching and learning, and provides them

---

8   Future Leaders Trust, Heads up: meeting the challenges of headteacher recruitment, Future Leaders Trust, 2016, p.10

with a 'safety net', a mentor, and time to reflect.'

Apart from executive headship and the heads of individual schools, there are many other leadership roles in MATs. A key role is that of business manager or chief operating officer, who may well also be company secretary and responsible for servicing the board of trustees. Where schools are making the most of their partnership, other school leaders, middle managers and subject experts will also be working beyond their own school. Raising achievement across a MAT involves more school-to-school support work than just helping schools in difficulty. A MAT literacy co-ordinator, for example, will work with all schools in the MAT to improve the teaching, learning and assessment work in that area of the curriculum and to support all staff in bringing their practice up to the level of the best.

Building a successful MAT

In a blog post, Robert Hill wrote about how groups of schools can create systems for school improvement.[9] *'The best chains,'* he wrote, *'have thought about, evolved and systemised their approach to school improvement.'* His ten points are instructive for anyone planning to build an effective partnership of schools and should be read in full. They can be summarised as follows:

1. **They know their academies well quantitatively.** In a culture of high expectations, demanding targets are set and progress and performance are monitored. A standard core data set is developed and used, in different forms, with teachers, school leaders and board members. There is a clear and consistent performance management framework for academies, leaders and staff.

2. **They know their academies well qualitatively.** This goes beyond the metrics to an understanding of how progress is or is not being made. Senior and middle leaders develop a shared approach to lesson observations and conduct joint learning walks. Academy leaders jointly investigate issues of common concern. External reviews are commissioned.

---

9   roberthilleducationblog.com/academy-chains/205/ This also appears on the Future Leaders website at www.future-leaders.org.uk/insights-blog/school-improvement-multi-academy-trusts/ See also Robert Hill et al, The growth of academy chains: implications for leaders and leadership, National College for School Leadership, 2012

3. **They adapt strategies to an academy's context.** The best MATs understand where each academy is on its school improvement journey and have identified the issues needing to be addressed, mobilising resources to tackle weaknesses. Good MAT leadership adapts interventions to maintain momentum as improvement takes place.[10]

4. **They deploy expertise strategically.** MATs give their best and emerging leaders experience of leadership by deploying them to support schools with particular issues. They also identify expertise across the MAT and use it wherever it is needed. This approach both makes use of expertise and also helps to retain staff who might otherwise look for new challenges elsewhere.[11]

5. **They coach improvement in teaching and learning.** Many MATs use coaching to improve teaching, learning and assessment. The coaching model may use pairs or triads, real-time feedback or video technology. Thorough training of the coaches is essential, as is the engagement of all staff in the coaching process.

6. **They use enquiry-based learning as the flywheel to accelerate improvement.** In inquiry-based learning, staff learn with and from each other, both within and between schools, about what makes an impact on student learning and progress. Professional development of this type is much deeper than attending training courses, incorporating means such as lesson study, action research, and joint curriculum and lesson planning.

7. **They empower their middle leaders.** Successful groups of schools maximise the leadership input of their middle leaders, getting them to work together within and between schools. Distributed leadership, as we saw in chapter 8, includes more than the members of the senior leadership team. Middle leaders can be asked to lead whole-school, or even whole-MAT, reform projects, such as closing attainment gaps.

8. **They evolve and apply some non-negotiables.** Most MATs have common financial and data systems, as well as shared school policies and human resources management. Where a school is doing badly, approaches to

---

10 See also Peter Matthews, Simon Rea, Robert Hill and Qing Gu, Freedom to lead: a study of outstanding primary school leadership in England, National College for Teaching and Leadership, 2014 www.gov.uk/government/uploads/system/uploads/attachment_data/file/363794/RR374A_-_Outstanding_primaries_final_report.pdf

11 The first appointment after the CEO in the MAT where I am a trustee was of a mathematics coordinator, emphasising the MAT's focus on school improvement.

teaching and classroom management may be centrally imposed. As MATs mature and draw on the best practice within the group, common approaches to pedagogy may emerge. Co-construction between teachers and leaders across academies is key to this process.

9. **They work with and learn from other schools.** Leaders of successful MATs are outward-looking in their search for evidence of good practice and they will extend this approach to staff across all schools in the group.

10. **They know their impact.** High-performing MATs are able to demonstrate the impact they are making on improving schools within the trust – one of the key issues Ofsted looks for when it inspects MATs. In addition, they understand the impact of specific interventions. They also evaluate the health and organisational maturity of the MAT itself using, perhaps, one of the MAT frameworks or checklists developed by Future Leaders or the regional schools commissioners.

Robert Hill's blog post continued with five attributes important for leaders of multi-academy trusts or other groups of schools:

'*They are **respectful** of the identity and character of individual academies and of a school's strengths, as well as understanding where it needs to make improvement.*

*They are **resourceful** in that they do whatever it takes and mobilise the support needed to bring about improvement.*

*They are **responsive** to the context of each academy and its particular needs and adapt their strategies as circumstances change.*

*They are **relentless** in their pursuit of improvement and adopt a 'no excuses' approach – believing that every child can achieve.*

*They are **resilient** in persevering with improvement despite challenges and setbacks.*'

In the Learn Academies Trust in Market Harborough, the CEO, Stef Edwards, worked with the heads of the other schools to plan the way in which the Trust would operate when it started in September 2016. Using the above approach, she produced an audit and planning tool in a table stating what we should do and how we could do it. Each of the ten points above was tabulated against the current position in the schools and how we could build on existing practice and create capacity in each area. This approach provides a good basis for future strategic planning.

Although RSCs are concentrating their efforts on brokering new structural arrangements for schools deemed to be under-performing and this is reflected in David Carter's plans for the growth of MATs, David's strong moral purpose, which was evident in his leadership of the Cabot Learning Federation of schools in the Bristol area, is focused on school improvement and improving the life chances of young people. There is little point for school leaders in all the hard work of conversion to academy status and the formation of MATs unless this leads to an improvement in education for the learners.

MATs have beneficially created new models of governance and leadership, greater opportunities for staff professional development, more efficient use of resources and more purposeful collaboration between schools, but the evidence is not yet clear on the most significant element – the extent to which MATs raise the attainment of learners. The challenge for school leaders is to ensure that the work of MATs produces that improvement, both in terms of test and examination results and in the opportunities available to learners.

Teaching schools

Teaching schools have had six areas of activity – initial teacher training, professional and leadership development, talent management and succession planning, school-to-school support, specialist leaders of education, and research and development – although these are often treated as three or four themes, rather than six. In an evaluation of teaching schools[12] published in 2015, a research team (of which I was a member) reported that there is a wide variety of operating structures and priorities across the 600 teaching schools in England, which are influenced by the values and visions of teaching school leaders, as well as by different histories of partnership and culture.

The report noted that teaching school alliances and MATs serve different purposes, with different organisational structures and accountability arrangements. Whereas MATs have tight accountability structures, with boards of trustees and local governing bodies, teaching schools have more fluid accountability arrangements, which generally rely on the teaching school leaders working together to build collaboration and social capital across the alliance.

The study found a continuing appetite among school leaders to apply for teaching school status, seen by leaders as hugely time-consuming but worthwhile. Leadership credibility, trustworthiness and resilience were viewed as paramount in building and leading teaching school alliances.

NLEs are headteachers who support schools in difficulty. They lead outstanding schools, which are designated as national support schools (NSS). A 2006

---

12   Qing Gu et al, Teaching schools evaluation: final report, National College for Teaching and Leadership, 2015

White Paper had proposed that the most outstanding headteachers should be designated as national leaders of education, intended by ministers to be a badge of success and bringing with it various privileges, such as attendance at consultation meetings in Whitehall. However, the secretary of state asked Steve Munby, CEO of the National College, to convene a group to develop the NLE role. The group's recommendations were that designation as an NLE should be a school improvement role, not just a badge of success, and that NLEs should forfeit the title if they did not carry out support work in other schools. Crucially, the group recognised that a school's success is not just about the quality of the head and proposed that these outstanding schools that were engaged in school-to-school support work should be given the title of national support schools. The secretary of state accepted the recommendations.

In addition, local authorities designated some heads of successful schools as local leaders of education (LLEs) and the National College subsequently extended the number of support roles to include national leaders of governance (NLGs) and specialist leaders of education (SLEs).

The evaluation report stated that ITT, CPD and school-to-school support were seen by teaching school leaders as the key strands of their work. The deployment of NLEs, LLEs, SLEs and NLGs to support other schools provides many leadership opportunities for successful staff.

The SLE category provides welcome recognition for excellent senior and middle leaders, who do a large amount of the school-to-school support work carried out through teaching schools. In trying to influence school-to-school support policy in the 2000s, I reminded ministers and officials many times that there are more good parts of schools than there are good schools, so school improvement policy should be structured in a way that enables the system to benefit from the expertise of individuals and teams who do not necessarily work in the outstanding schools that become national support schools or teaching schools. The designation of SLEs has enabled these people, whose expertise ranges from science to business management, and from special needs to behaviour management, to be utilised for the good of the system.

Paul Stone, the director of the Affinity teaching school alliance in Leicestershire, which has over 60 primary schools in membership, is clear about both the opportunities and the challenges for teaching schools. They are a mechanism that creates many more leadership opportunities than exist in individual schools, particularly in the primary sector. In addition to the opportunities for NLEs, LLEs, NLGs and SLEs to be involved in school-to-school support, this work includes the leadership of training from initial teacher training through to headship preparation and executive leadership, as well as networks at all levels.

Within the Affinity alliance, there are several MATs, whose leaders see the alliance as offering broader opportunities than can be provided by an individual MAT. The National College study found that the biggest challenge for teaching schools is sustainability and Paul agrees that financial management and an innovative approach to income generation are essential for leaders of successful alliances. However, he believes that this risk is mitigated by MATs collaborating within the alliance, offering and buying into each other's services. With the reduction in LA capacity, Affinity has developed an education psychology service, which MATs buy into, while individual MATs have developed other services, so provision across the alliance is complementary.

Like all the most successful teaching school alliances, Affinity has nurtured an increasing degree of trust between the alliance and individual MATs and schools, thus breaking down some of the barriers of competition between schools. This requires an openness between school leaders, sharing their growth plans and concerns, and is a good basis to develop knowledge sharing across the alliance's headteacher and MAT CEO networks.

Skills and attributes needed for leadership beyond the school

In the NCSL report on executive headship (2010), the surveyed heads identified eight skills needed for this role:

1. Operating at a more strategic level

2. Getting the balance between standardisation and respecting difference

3. Being even-handed between schools

4. Staying focused on performance

5. Developing and practising interpersonal skills

6. Working closely with governors

7. Communicating effectively

8. Developing personal resilience

All 12 of the leadership behaviours discussed in chapter 8 are used by executive heads and those working in other roles outside the school. Some of these, such as distributed leadership, outward-looking leadership and communicative leadership are arguably even more important for wider leadership roles, but all feature strongly in the armoury of school leaders working in more than one school.

The NFER/NGA/Future Leaders report stated that:[13]

---

13   Lord, P et al, op.cit., 2016, pp.19-20

'Consistent with other literature, we found in this study that executive headteachers need to be resilient, optimistic, emotionally intelligent, determined, decisive, creative and have a strong moral purpose and passion to improve the life chances of children through education. ... We found that, in many ways, the skills that executive headteachers need are similar to those necessary for a more traditional role. Both executive heads and headteachers need to think strategically, communicate effectively, support others to develop, build effective teams and be well organised. However, the executive head role requires individuals to demonstrate these skills at a higher level.'

The application of leadership skills and behaviours varies as the MAT moves from establishment to development to maturity, and leaders have to be flexible in their approach over time. Most of the skills required by executive heads are also needed by other school leaders engaged in school-to-school support work and they too should adapt their approach as their work in other schools develops and the resulting changes in practice become embedded.

Growing opportunities

While the pendulum of education policy has swung back and forth in so many ways, there has been a steady growth, encouraged by ministers of all political parties, in the breadth and depth of roles for school leaders beyond their own school. Many of these roles are listed in figure 11.

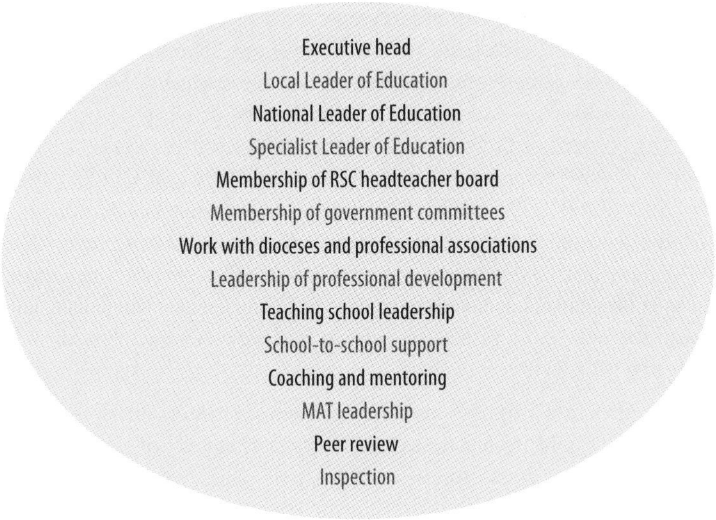

Executive head
Local Leader of Education
National Leader of Education
Specialist Leader of Education
Membership of RSC headteacher board
Membership of government committees
Work with dioceses and professional associations
Leadership of professional development
Teaching school leadership
School-to-school support
Coaching and mentoring
MAT leadership
Peer review
Inspection

Figure 11 Wider leadership roles, 2016

177

As we saw in chapter 5, organisations such as Challenge Partners, the Education Development Trust, the SSAT in its redesigned form, Whole Education and other bodies, including some LAs, carry out peer reviews, bringing an external perspective to a school and outward-facing opportunities for the leaders who are reviewing as well as those whose work is being reviewed. In addition, the chief inspector, Sir Michael Wilshaw, has accelerated the trend for inspection teams to include serving school senior and middle leaders, which is normal practice on independent school inspections.

The DfE has primary and secondary headteacher reference groups, comprising around 15 heads on each, which, according the DfE website, 'act as a confidential sounding board, advising on the potential impact of policies on primary and secondary education, including any barriers to implementation'. Other groups, such as those focused on workload and bureaucracy, also involve school leaders in the DfE's work. The Teaching Schools Council, comprising regional representatives of teaching school leaders, is regularly consulted by the DfE and NCTL.

One of the most welcome recent developments is that the government now routinely appoints headteachers to key national roles and committees, which would have been hard to imagine at the turn of the century. Sir Michael Wilshaw as chief inspector and Sir David Carter as national schools commissioner are two prominent examples of successful heads moving into major national jobs. Government reviews have often been chaired by heads, such as Sir Andrew Carter, head of South Farnham School, who led the review of the quality and effectiveness of initial teacher training; Stephen Munday, CEO of the Comberton Academy Trust in Cambridgeshire, who chaired the review of the content of ITT courses; Dame Dana Ross-Wawrzynski, executive headteacher of Altrincham Grammar School for Girls and CEO of the Bright Futures Educational Trust, who led the review of headteacher standards; Dame Sally Coates who led a review of education in prison; Dame Reena Keeble, a retired primary head, who is leading a review of effective practices in primary schools; and Ian Bauckham, executive head of the Bennett Memorial Diocesan School and former ASCL president, who is leading a review of modern foreign languages teaching.

This surely represents a sign of confidence in school leaders and a recognition of the value they bring to policy-making. However, this level of early consultation with school leaders does not always happen and, when the government announces new policies without first taking the views of leading professionals, the shortcomings of the policy are usually revealed quickly, as was the case with the green paper in September 2016 on the extension of grammar schools.

Co-ordinating school improvement

Traditionally, the local authority, which had statutory responsibility for the quality of schools in its area, provided school improvement services. These were of varying quality across the 150 LAs in England and 22 in Wales. As discussed in chapter 2, the 2016 White Paper set out a new three-part role for LAs, which did not include school improvement.

Although ministers have gradually written local authorities out of the school improvement script, many LAs still play a role in this area. In Cumbria, for example, the heads work with the LA in the Cumbria Association of System Leaders; in Cambridgeshire, the LA hosts meetings with the group of local teaching schools to decide how school-to-school support could best be delivered to schools in need of it; in South Gloucestershire, the LA facilitates an Education Partnership Board (on which I serve as independent chair) to co-ordinate school improvement activities. These are all LAs which have recognised the shape of the new landscape of schools in their area and have developed a new relationship with school leaders, which is more of an equal partnership than was the case in the past, when LA personnel too often considered the LA to be far above schools in the local educational hierarchy.

LA approaches vary from an attempt to continue with the traditional model of services and staff provided by the LA, with schools signing service-level agreements, to an approach in which schools form self-improving local clusters and take ownership of school improvement in their area. Local authority adviser support is a feature of the traditional model, while quality assurance is generally pursued through peer review in other models. Some LAs have formed a partnership company in which school leaders serve on the board. In most models, LAs exercise a monitoring function, providing data support and identifying vulnerable schools. The nature of links between the LA and teaching schools in its area is critical in providing timely support for schools in difficulty.

Local historical and political factors play a part in the decision as to which model is adopted in each LA. Other critical factors include leadership capacity in the schools and the proportion of schools with academy status, although there is an increasing number of areas in which academies work well with the LA and with other schools.

As the school system in England has increasingly become nationally organised, with academies having a direct relationship with the DfE and its funding arm, the Education Funding Agency (EFA), the local government role has waned. If the 2016 White Paper is implemented, the LA role will become clearer, but the move to mass academisation means that school improvement arrangements will continue to evolve.

Some LAs have already reduced their school improvement staff from around 60 personnel to two or three and it is possible that some of these LAs will eventually withdraw from education altogether, apart from a small number of statutory obligations. Regional, or sub-regional, organisations would make sense in some parts of the country, especially where there are city mayors. There are 32 LAs in London, but the mayor has an education department and Boris Johnson, the mayor from 2008 to 2016, wanted to expand his education domain. What is certain is that school improvement benefits from a strong local partnership between the LA and schools, with school leaders playing a leading role. Only where school leaders are prepared to take on this wider responsibility and deploy their most effective staff to support other schools is the system likely to thrive.

The way forward for leadership in a school-led self-improving system

In 2010, David Hargreaves wrote powerfully about the creation of a self-improving system[14], setting out a vision of *'a new era in which the school system becomes the major agent of its own improvement,'* with four drivers of this change:

- Strong clusters: groups of schools working together, sharing resources and expertise
- Local solutions across groups: local self-evaluation leading to local action
- Raising aspirations across the whole area
- Building leadership capacity across groups of schools

At a later seminar at the National College, David Hargreaves set out four keys to the deep partnerships that he believed were required for a self-improving school system:

- Joint practice development – more significant than traditional professional development and sharing what does not work as well as what does
- High social capital – building trust through reciprocity, and vice versa, creating a virtuous circle
- Collective moral purpose – shared values across groups and more widely across the system

---

14 David H Hargreaves, Creating a self-improving system, National College for School Leadership, 2010

- Evaluation and challenge – peer-based, and backed by high social capital and collective moral purpose

The development of teaching schools and multi-academy trusts, alongside wider leadership roles, has provided the structural framework within which school leaders have been given increased opportunities to put into practice the points made here by David Hargreaves.

The report of the Academies Commission, established by Pearson and the Royal Society of Arts in 2012, found that academisation had injected vitality into schools and recognised three imperatives for academies as their number grows in a self-improving system:

- *'to ensure that there is a forensic focus on teaching and its impact on pupils' learning so that the gap between the vision for academies and practice in classrooms is reduced*

- *to ensure that an increasingly academised system is fair and equally accessible to children and young people from all backgrounds*

- *to ensure that academies demonstrate their moral purpose and professionalism by providing greater accountability to pupils, parents and other stakeholders. The role of governors is more important than ever in an academised system, and their scrutiny and challenge should ensure effective accountability.'* [15]

The main responsibility for putting these imperatives into action lies with academy leaders, but the point about governors is a reminder of their importance in a system which has fewer checks and balances than when schools operated within local authorities.

As Toby Greany concluded from his analysis of the four policy scenarios, quoted in chapter 8, the system needs more policy consistency and more time to develop the deep partnerships, mentioned by David Hargreaves, that will meet the needs of every school and every child. These are in place already in some parts of the country, but not in others. While the government can incentivise partnership-working, it will be up to school leaders to take the lead in planning, developing, nurturing and bringing to maturity partnerships of schools that will stand the test of time. There is plenty of successful practice on which to draw, if the independence of academies is to be balanced in a positive way by interdependence between schools working in groups.

As Andreas Schleicher, the head of education at the OECD, said at the launch

---

15   Unleashing greatness: Getting the best from an academised system, the Report of the Academies Commission, Pearson RSA, 2013

of the Academies Commission report, the world's best school systems are those with a high level of school autonomy – but so are some of the worst. Only when autonomy is given to schools in a system that incentivises collaboration does it deliver success across the system as a whole.

School leaders need the government to be clear about which of Greany's four scenarios it is pursuing. A more coherent government vision for reform, clearly focused on supporting the development of a self-improving system that includes all schools and gives due weight to both independence and interdependence, is urgently needed. As stated in chapter 2, it would be healthier for the system as a whole if the political aim of increased *diversity and choice* were replaced by the aim of *high standards through autonomy in a climate of collaboration.*

In a collaborative school system, it is inevitable that some competition will still exist between schools, each wanting to provide the best education for its learners. Collaboration and competition can co-exist, provided school leaders recognise that, as co-leaders of education in their area, the most important outcome is how well the school system does for all children in the locality, not how each individual school performs. School leaders need to pursue this aim actively together and become the creators of the collaborative landscape in which all can flourish.

As John Hattie pointed out in the quotation in chapter 2, failure on the part of school leaders to do this will ensure that autonomy leads to a hierarchy of schools, in which the strong will flourish and the weak will become weaker. Toby Greany believes that the government's approach is so confused that it creates the risk of a two-tier system, in which confident and successful schools and leaders thrive, but the remainder feel constrained and do not have the capacity to self-improve.

It is good that ASCL, NAHT and the Education Development Trust (formerly CfBT) have joined together to host the Inspiring Leadership conference each summer in Birmingham, after the National College had decided to abandon it. As the leaders of the three organisations said in a joint article: *'The simple fact is that educational reform must come to be defined less by politicians and much more by the profession itself. We must own it.'* [16]

ASCL and NAHT, representing over 50,000 school leaders, have a particularly good opportunity to lead system reform, with the voices of the leaders of academy chains, MATs and teaching schools potentially influential within

---

16   Russell Hobby, Brian Lightman and Steve Munby, 'Say it loud: leaders of our schools, unite!', Times Educational Supplement, 6 June 2014

both organisations. The ASCL blueprint of a self-improving system[17] was widely welcomed, both by politicians and by professionals, and represents an agenda around which there could be a degree of consensus about the way forward.

The Teaching Schools Council also has an important role to play in influencing the shape and direction of the system, as has the Headteachers Round Table, which was formed by a proactive cross-sector group of heads in 2012 and which publishes policy papers.

The role of school leaders beyond their own schools extends to the co-leadership of the education system. It is profoundly to be hoped that politicians are prepared to work with the grain of the views of school leaders, and not let professional expertise be trumped by frequently changing political priorities.

Challenges for a school-led self-improving system

Policy tensions. As discussed in chapter 8, there are considerable tensions inherent in government policy on schools. Some policies promote collaboration and partnership-working, while others add to the many policies that have, over three decades, encouraged competition between schools and made it harder for schools to work together.

Nowhere is this more evident than in the area of admissions, where academies are their own admissions authorities, subject to the judgements of the Office of the Schools Adjudicator. It cannot be good for whole-system success that thousands of schools are allowed to make their own decisions about whom they admit. As in other countries, deciding on the allocation of school places is surely a task for the local authority.

An increase in selection. The government green paper in September 2016[18], advocating an increase in grammar schools, will, if implemented, create a major challenge for collaborative partnerships between schools in selective areas, as is already experienced in areas where there are grammar schools. The secretary of state, Justine Greening, has said that the new grammar schools, which she described as being 'inclusive', should play a part in local MATs. However, grammar schools are, by definition, exclusive and it is hard to see how they will strengthen partnership working.

Pressure for rapid change. The political pressure on schools in difficulty to improve rapidly can be understood in the context of children having only

---

17   Association of School and College Leaders, Leading the way: blueprint for a self-improving system, ASCL, 2015
18   Department for Education, Schools that work for everyone: Government consultation, HMSO, 2016

one chance of a good education; if improvement is slow, the young people in the school at the time will continue to be disadvantaged. However, in order to make sustainable change to schools in this position, support mechanisms need to be in place over a considerable period. There have been too many cases of 'superheads' 'turning around' 'failing schools' (to use three terms that are misleading, but have become common parlance in the political discourse about schools in challenging situations) and then leaving before the changes have become fully embedded.

Sustainable change, which in the end is more cost-effective, usually takes several years and includes change of culture, as well as of systems, to ensure that success is sustained through improved teaching, learning and assessment.

The problems left behind after rapid in-and-out interventions caused several of the early school improvement schemes, such as 'fresh start', to flounder. Where schools are in a group with sufficient leadership capacity to provide ongoing support, this can be avoided, although considerable leadership and financial resources have to be consistently applied.[19]

Forced academisation. The best partnerships are those where relationships have been built over time by school leaders and there is a high degree of interdependence between schools. Adequate leadership capacity is also required. If problems in a school in a MAT are identified at a sufficiently early stage, the leadership of the MAT will broker support from another school in the MAT, a local teaching school or from further afield. Support may even be found within the school itself, with an outstanding head of mathematics supporting a struggling head of science, for example.

However, particularly if the school itself is unable or unwilling to identify its deficiencies, an external agency has to work with the school to decide what is in need of improvement. Increasingly, this identification is carried out by an academy chain or the lead school in a MAT. In more extreme cases – failing an inspection, consistently poor results, a major safeguarding issue or financial impropriety – the RSC will become involved. When the RSC is the broker of support, the solution is likely to be structural, putting the school into a new trust and often replacing the headteacher. This can create a difficult situation for other senior and middle leaders remaining in the school, who may well need to learn new leadership skills and how to apply them in order to improve the school's performance.

---

19   Alex Hill et al, 'The one type of leader who can turn around a failing school', Harvard Business Review, October 2016, hbr.org/2016/10/the-one-type-of-leader-who-can-turn-around-a-failing-school

The supply of headteachers and executive heads. The vulnerability of headteachers has been growing in line with the increase in accountability and the political pressure on schools to improve. This has undoubtedly contributed to an increase in negative perceptions about headship, with 87 per cent of school leaders reported as saying that headship was less attractive in 2015 than in 2010.[20] Women are still under-represented in headship and the proportion of black and minority ethnic heads remains woefully small.

Meanwhile, demand for headteachers is likely to increase with the number of free schools planned to open. Demand for executive heads too will undoubtedly increase, with Sir David Carter encouraging the rapid growth of MATs and the NFER/NGA/Future Leaders report, which also took retirements into account, estimating that there could be demand for between 3203 and 6786 additional executive heads in the future.[21] This represents a massive challenge for school leadership development and recruitment.

Recruitment of the next generation of heads is not something to be left to the government. Creating a sufficient number of talented potential leaders is a challenge that school leaders, individually and collectively, must meet.

Maintaining improvement. In challenging school environments, school improvement is not easy to achieve and more than 150 academies have been issued by RSCs with 'warning notices'. These can be issued for three reasons: when results are 'unacceptably low'; when there has been a 'serious breakdown' in school management or governance; or when the safety of learners is threatened. Over 100 academies have been re-brokered by RSCs from one sponsor to another and more than 40 trusts have been issued with financial notices to improve.

Developing and maintaining partnership arrangements between schools places a considerable burden on school leaders and governing boards. The potential of collaboration to raise student achievement is great, but the aim of partnerships must always be clearly focused on school improvement.

Responsible financial management. Financial propriety is a prime obligation on school leaders and governing boards. In the grant-maintained system in the 1980s and 1990s, the Funding Agency for Schools had a rigorous system of audit to which every GM school was subjected. According to the *TES*,[22] the Education

---

20   Future Leaders Trust, Heads up: meeting the challenges of headteacher recruitment, Future Leaders, 2016. The survey result was taken from The Key, State of education survey report, 2015.

21   Op cit., p.22.

22   Times Educational Supplement, 9 September 2016

Funding Agency (EFA) has not been able to exercise the same level of financial oversight on the large number of academies and MATs, with a majority of its investigations into financial impropriety being triggered by whistleblowers rather than by the EFA's own checking systems. These have attracted a good deal of attention in the media, especially where the trust leader has been a high-profile figure, and some cases have gone to court.

There were cases of financial impropriety and fraud in schools before academies were invented, but the extent of financial autonomy has increased with the growth of academies and MATs and this places a particular responsibility for probity on school leaders and trustees.

The need for MATs to collaborate with each other. With over 70 per cent of academies in single academy trusts and well over 90 per cent in MATs with fewer than six schools, the cohesion of the system will, to a great extent, depend not only on the strength of co-operation within MATs, but how well separate MATs work together. The co-ordinating power of the RSCs will be important, but more important still will be the wider moral purpose of executive heads, headteachers and governing boards to work for the common good. The alternative is that schools will use their autonomy to return to the competition between schools that dominated the GM era, with winners and losers in a steeper hierarchy of schools, and some children and communities paying the price.

***

With a wide range of opportunities open to school leaders to work beyond their own school, the leadership of school improvement across the system is increasingly in the hands of successful school leaders, with senior and middle leaders and chairs of governing boards providing school-to-school support in many places.

As the number of academies grows, from 200 sponsored academies in 2010 to nearly 6000 sponsored and convertor academies in 2016, the school system in England has become much more fragmented. However, the extension of collaborative structures from the chains of sponsored academies that emerged before 2010, to the widespread and increasing number of MATs, has produced a new, more purposeful, style of partnership working among school leaders.

There is a growing body of work on the leadership of successful school partnerships and both MATs and teaching school alliances have the potential to transform the landscape of schools in England in a positive way.

Although the skills and behaviours of school leadership outlined in chapter 8 remain essential for those carrying out work outside their own school, some leadership characteristics are especially important. The application of these will need to vary as partnership-working moves towards maturity.

In a confusing policy climate, where collaboration and competition, and autonomy and central direction, co-exist in often uncomfortable juxtaposition, there is nonetheless a discernible trend towards a school-led self-improving system. MATs and teaching schools provide the structure in which school leaders can use their skills and experience to improve the quality of education for young people well beyond their own institution. Such a school-led system also places an obligation on all school leaders, and especially headteachers, to be co-leaders of education in their area. The direction of the system feels more than ever to be in the hands of school leaders.

Chapter 10

Conclusion: school leadership in context

Success is a journey, not a destination.
Arthur Ashe

Planning the journey

The recurring theme of this book has been the way in which values-led leadership can open up opportunities for students and staff and build a high-achieving school with a clear sense of direction. With values underpinning decision-making and with an innovative approach to policy and practice, it is possible, even with a high degree of central government control, to steer a steady path for the school and not be blown off course by the pressure of external factors.

This approach to school leadership requires leaders constantly to articulate the school's agreed vision and values, using every opportunity to put them into practice. It means that the leaders take ownership of the school's agenda, so the school develops its own ethos and characteristics; provides a values-led curriculum fit for the 21st century; embeds assessment into teaching and learning; uses accountability to reinforce the school's priorities, setting school-based accountability measures; raises attainment for all learners, but especially the disadvantaged, in ways that increase social mobility and close the attainment gap; creates a learning climate and works towards joint practice development. It means never saying, 'we did it for Ofsted', but focusing constantly on the needs and aspirations of the learners and the opportunities that can be created for them.

School leaders are working in a policy climate full of confusion, with the political rhetoric of autonomy and its manifestation in academies and free schools contrasting with unprecedented (in terms of the history of schools in England) control by government, as policies of centralisation and decentralisation, and collaboration and competition, threaten constantly to pull school leaders in opposite directions.

There has been a more consistent trend from autocratic leadership to more distributed leadership, not least because of the increase in the breadth of responsibilities placed on school leaders and governing boards by government legislation and regulation. This has been paralleled by the trend away from leadership focused almost entirely on a single school to co-leadership of the school system.

Finding a way through the policy confusion clears the path for school leaders not only to give consistent leadership to their schools, but to play a strong part as co-leaders of education in the locality and, increasingly, to have a significant role in the leadership of the national education system.

In the amount of autonomy and breadth of decision-making, and the potential for innovation and creativity, school leadership in the UK is envied in the many other countries where central and local district government control of schools is at a level not seen in England and Wales since 1988. 'Bog-standard' may be a truthful description of schools in countries where there is little room for individual school innovation, but it is certainly not the case in England, where school leadership has never been one-dimensional. The local context and history of a school contribute to its uniqueness and provide the platform on which school leaders and staff can develop an institution that maximises the life chances of every young person.

'Diversity and choice' have been the underlying policy themes of successive governments, which they have interpreted as the creation of different types of secondary school. This pursuit of diversity has contributed to a steeper hierarchy of schools, which has served the interests of learners in schools that are near the bottom of the pecking-order very badly.

Instead of 'diversity between schools', 'diversity within schools' should be the aim of policy. The capacity of schools in the UK to develop their own ethos and characteristics enables 'diversity within' to be provided. Good comprehensive secondary schools, like their primary counterparts, provide diversity within the school to meet the varied abilities and aspirations of the learners. Where there is a high level of standardisation between what schools offer, this is mostly because of the government-imposed curriculum, accountability measures, tests and examinations.

A wider context

The multiple roles of each teacher and school leader make it difficult to look beyond the constantly changing world of education, with its frequent policy announcements and resurrections of the sterile debates of the past, to the wider field of public service.

As school leaders consider the implications of tighter budgets, increased accountability and new regulations, it is easy to forget that these issues are being faced by the leaders of other public services too. In health, social services, probation, crime prevention, transport, culture, environment and local government, employees, and particularly leaders, face the same range of pressures as education leaders – increased public scrutiny and media interest, changing and often unintelligent accountability measures, increasing demands and reduced funding.

This creates similar tensions for leaders of all public services and demands a fresh look at the way in which public services are governed. In a paper for the Centre for Public Impact, Sir Peter Housden sets out the issues and suggests a constructive way forward.[1] Peter's background as a history teacher, chief education officer, local authority chief executive, director-general of schools in the DfE and permanent secretary, latterly as head of the civil service in Scotland, gives him a broad perspective well-rooted in his first-hand experience of schools and education policy. He concludes that, while there is agreement on the importance of excellence and equity, and recognition of the impact of demographic change and information technology, *'thinking and practice on improvement and reform in public services are in urgent need of renewal.'*

He states that the right of government to set levels of ambition, articulate its priorities and hold services to account should be respected, and sets three criteria against which reform of public services should be judged:

- *'It must sustain public confidence.*
- *It must command the respect and affiliation of the broad mass of practitioners as their sustained creativity and commitment will be essential if the challenges of the current moment are to be surmounted.*
- *It needs to be coherent and provide a reliable guide to those involved in the leadership and stewardship of services and in the development of policy at all levels.'*

---

1   Peter Housden, Rethinking public services, Centre for Public Impact, 2016

Although he believes that much has been achieved, including the empowerment of frontline leaders, he finds it apparent that:

- *'Closely-monitored, high-stakes accountability against narrow performance measures is not a tool for effective system-wide management.*

- *Quasi-market mechanisms were expected to generate momentum for improvement in service quality, but ... improvements in service standards remain patchy. There has been no transition 'from good to great', with significant difficulty in the recruitment and retention of high-quality staff.'*

Peter Housden believes that:

'The appropriate foundation for a new paradigm lies not in a fresh theory of the state but in the lives of citizens. The unifying goal for public services should be to enable citizens to be, and remain, in charge of their own lives.

This implies a profound shift in our thinking and practice. It requires an approach to mobilise the citizen's energy in the drive to secure personal autonomy – the process known as co-production.'

The implications for school leadership in this approach are clear. School leaders need to work increasingly with learners and parents in ways that give them an even greater investment in the school's success. In chapter 5, the need for improved accountability to parents was discussed as a positive factor in school leadership, while in chapter 8, the need for excellent communications with parents was stressed.

Equally, the government needs to work more constructively and at a deeper level with school leaders and teachers in developing the education service. *'Co-production,'* according to Peter Housden, *'is a collaborative process enjoining the citizen and practitioner. Practitioners should become co-authors of public service improvement.'* Thus the government needs to take a step back and create the space for this effective co-production, respecting institutional autonomy and the need for collaboration to build on the success of leading practitioners, thus generating momentum of reform from within the service.

Linking policy and implementation

This is certainly not happening in the government of education in England. As we saw particularly in chapters 3 and 4, the extent of curriculum and examinations reform places unreasonable expectations on teachers and is unfair to the learners going through the system. As professionals constantly seeking improvement in the quality of the service they provide, teachers would not resist change if they felt greater ownership of it, discussed in the context of servant leadership in chapter 8. However, much of the government's reform programme is top-down change of the worst kind, without any regard to implementation.

The key to successful government of education, as in other public services, is the link between policy and implementation. The late Steve Marshall, an Australian who was head of education for the Welsh government in Cardiff, wrote: '*You often find in education systems that, when policy is determined, implementation is not always considered to the degree it could be and principals will say "If only you had asked us ..."*'

The government has a democratic mandate to introduce policies and school leaders and teachers are the professional experts who hold the key to implementation. The policies cannot succeed unless the implementation is good – and for that, ministers and civil servants need to talk to the professionals before introducing legislation or new policies.

This co-production would be perfectly possible if the DfE were to talk to the representatives of school leaders earlier in the policy-making process and extend the remit of the primary and secondary headteacher reference groups.

We are a long way from this scenario. It is as if the 24-hour news cycle needs to be fed a constant diet of education stories, showing that the government is impatient to reform every aspect of the education system. While schools are implementing the last few changes, the next are already being announced. No successful business could be run on this basis.

In order to operate most effectively, school leaders require a new alignment to be forged between the government and schools. Strong, autonomous schools must be empowered to collaborate, and held to account intelligently within a framework in which autonomy, collaboration and accountability are in a new, more productive balance – top-down empowerment with bottom-up development. Co-production will evolve most successfully through an enabling government working with an innovative profession.

In Housden's new paradigm, the government retains its strategic role, prioritising policies and holding schools to account intelligently. After the torrent of legislation, regulation and new direction, it will take time for the DfE to regain the respect and confidence of the leaders of the profession, so that they implement with enthusiasm and commitment the more coherent programme of change for which the profession yearns.

Taking ownership

School leaders are driven by moral purpose to improve the lives of young people. They relish the daily opportunity to make a difference for the young.

They know that they have to be accountable, but they want to be trusted by the government, as surveys suggest that they are by children, parents and the public. It is surely time to move from a low trust, high accountability system to high trust, intelligent accountability policies.

In an interview with the *TES*,[2] the chief executive of the EEF, Sir Kevan Collins, asked:

'Are we running a system based on compliance or one based on professional trust? You can get a long way with compliance ... but that is not the same as the leaders who build professional trust through demonstrating that they know what the issues are; that they look far and wide for solutions; that they resource the changes well; that they evaluate the impact of what they do. It is the same outcome, but with forced compliance you get a tick-box compliance; with professional trust you get a deeper buy-in. To create great schools, you need the latter, not the former.'

This would encourage school leaders to emerge from the chrysalis of central government direction and take greater ownership and control of their school's future structure, curriculum development, assessment, accountability and professional training. The political rhetoric of autonomy cannot conceal the way in which the education workforce has been de-professionalised by continuous government-imposed changes. As Eleanor Roosevelt said in the 1930s: *'No one can make you feel inferior without your consent.'* The profession needs to get its confidence back, and it is up to school leaders to take the lead.

Andrew Morrish has written about the way in which he and the staff in his West Midlands primary school MAT have responded to this challenge and, in his book, *The art of standing out*,[3] he suggests that school leaders should look at their school through three lenses, which chime with the themes of this book:

- *The calibration lens*, to ensure that the school leaders' moral compass is pointing in the right direction
- *The kaleidoscopic lens*, to allow leaders to focus on creativity and innovation
- *The telescopic lens*, to look outwards to excellent practice elsewhere

Individually and collectively, school leaders need to take the lead in fighting for what they believe. If they are sufficiently confident in their expertise, they do not have to dance entirely to the government's tune.

Peter Hyman has contrasted the self-confident medical profession with a

---

2   Times Educational Supplement, 8 July 2016

3   Andrew Morrish, The art of standing out: school transformation, to greatness and beyond, John Catt, 2016, p.195

teaching profession that '*is in thrall to the government, reacting to the agenda set by politicians rather than having the self-confidence to promote its own priorities. With a more vibrant cohort of leaders and teachers than ever before, now is the time for us to show the backbone needed to create our own system. ... We have the expertise, the clout and the passion to design, shape and deliver a world class education system. We just need the will and the headspace to do what we know to be right.*' [4]

In particular, the way is open for school leaders to develop and build strong partnerships of schools, aspirational for every child, ambitious in standards of teaching, innovative in curriculum, rigorous in assessment, informed by evidence and with maximum opportunity for joint practice development. To give every child the opportunity of a high quality education, successful school leaders have a special responsibility to take less successful schools with them on this journey.

The opportunities for school leaders to change the lives of young people beneficially have never been greater, but the policy climate in which teachers work has never been more confusing. The ASCL *Blueprint*[5] shows how the leaders of the profession can play a more proactive role in policy-making. If the government, which welcomed the *Blueprint*, agrees to move forward in this way, it will be a major step in co-production between government and school leaders.

As we have seen at many points in this book, there is space for school leaders to be innovative and to set a clear direction for the school. Guided by a strong moral compass and the 12 leadership behaviours discussed in chapter 8, they can take ownership of the policy agenda, both for the benefit of their learners and for the good of the education system as a whole. Learning from others and sharing their successes, not only will learners achieve more, but this approach will help to make teaching into a stronger, more evidence-informed, more outward-looking profession. With principled and authentic leadership, firmly rooted in a set of agreed values, school leaders can take greater control, both locally and nationally, of the destiny of our education system.

In a world that feels more fragile than for a long time, with a crisis of confidence in traditional politics, the need for school leaders to take the lead in forging a great education system has never been more important.

---

4   Peter Hyman, 'The courage of our convictions' in Roy Blatchford and Rebecca Clark, Self-improving schools: the journey to excellence, John Catt, 2016

5   Association of School and College Leaders, Leading the way: blueprint for a self-improving system, ASCL, 2015

Select bibliography

Adonis A, *Education, education, education: Reforming England's schools,* Biteback, 2012

Assessment Reform Group, *The role of teachers in the assessment of learning,* 2004

Association of School and College Leaders, *Leading the way: Blueprint for a self-improving system,* ASCL, 2015

Baars S et al, *Lessons from London schools: Investigating the success,* CfBT, 2014

Bangs J, Macbeath J, and Galton M, *Reinventing schools, reforming teaching,* Routledge, 2011

Barber M, Donnelly K and Rizvi S, *Oceans of innovation: The Atlantic, the Pacific, global leadership and the future of education,* Institute for Public Policy Research, 2012

Black P and Wiliam D, *Inside the black box: Raising standards through classroom assessment,* King's College, London, 1998

Blatchford P et al, *The deployment and impact of support staff,* DCSF, 2009

Blatchford R, *The restless school,* John Catt, 2014

Blatchford R, *A practical guide: national standards of excellence for headteachers,* John Catt, 2015

Blatchford R and Clark R (eds.), *Self-improving schools: The journey to excellence,* John Catt, 2016

Brighouse T, *How successful head teachers survive and thrive,* Research Machines, 2010

Brown A, *The myth of the strong leader: Political leadership in the modern age,* Vintage, 2014

Buck A, *Leadership matters: How leaders at all levels can create great schools,* John Catt, 2016

Claxton G, *Building learning power,* TLO, 2002

Collins J, *Good to Great,* Random House, 2001

Confederation of British Industry, *First steps: A new approach for our schools,* CBI, 2012

Davies B and Brighouse T (eds.), *Passionate leadership in education,* Sage Publications, 2008

Department for Education and Skills, *14-19 Curriculum and qualifications reform: Final report of the Working Group on 14-19 reform,* HMSO, 2004

Department for Education, *National standards of excellence for headteachers: Departmental advice for headteachers, governing boards and aspiring headteachers,* HMSO, 2015

Department for Education, *Standard for teachers' professional development,* HMSO, 2016

Department for Education, *Schools that work for everyone: Government consultation,* HMSO, 2016

Dunford J, *Her Majesty's Inspectorate of schools since 1944: Standard bearers or turbulent priests?,* Woburn Press, 1998

Dunford J, *Review of the Office of the Children's Commissioner (England),* HMSO, 2010

Dunford J, Ten things learned on my leadership journey, 2011, https://johndunfordconsulting.wordpress.com/2011/11/01/ten-things-learned-on-my-leadership-journey/

Dunford J, Hill R, Parish N, and Rea S, *Establishing and leading new types of school,* National College for Teaching and Leadership, 2014

Fitch J, *Thomas and Matthew Arnold,* Heinemann, 1897

Future Leaders Trust, *Heads up: Meeting the challenges of headteacher recruitment,* Future Leaders, 2016

George B et al, 'Discovering Your Authentic Leadership', *Harvard Business Review,* February 2007

GL Assessment, *Pupil attitudes to self and school,* GL, 2016

Greany T, *The self-improving school system: Competing policies undermine the coalition's admirable aims,* Institute of Education blog, 6 March 2014

Greany T, *Self-improving school system: Will it be survival of the fittest or team effort?*, Institute of Education blog, 20 March 2014

Gu Q et al, *Teaching schools evaluation: Final report*, National College for Teaching and Leadership, 2015

Hargreaves A and Shirley D, *The fourth way*, Corwin Sage Publications, 2009

Hargreaves D H, *Creating a self-improving system*, National College for School Leadership, 2010

Hargreaves D H, *A self-improving school system: Towards maturity*, National College for School Leadership, 2012

Hattie J, *Visible learning*, Routledge, 2009

Hattie J, *What doesn't work in education: The politics of distraction*, Pearson, 2015

Higham R, Hopkins D, and Matthews P, *System leadership in practice*, McGraw Hill Open University Press, 2009

Hill R, *Achieving more together*, ASCL, 2008

Hill R et al, *The growth of academy chains: Implications for leaders and leadership*, National College for School Leadership, 2012

Hirsch E D, *Cultural literacy: What every American needs to know*, 1987

Hood M, *Beyond the plateau: The case for an Institute for Advanced Teaching*, IPPR, 2016

Hutchinson J and Dunford J, *Divergent pathways: The disadvantage gap, accountability and the pupil premium*, Education Policy Institute, 2016

Hopkins D, *Every school a great school: Realising the potential of system leadership*, McGraw Hill Open University Press, 2007

Housden P, *Rethinking public services*, Centre for Public Impact, 2016

King A and Crewe I, *The blunders of our governments*, Oneworld, 2013

Little A, *An intelligent person's guide to education*, Bloomsbury, 2015

Lord, P et al, *Executive headteachers: What's in a name? A full report of the findings*, NFER, NGA and the Future Leaders Trust, 2016

Macfarlane R and Wood D C (eds.), *Unleashing greatness*, London Leadership Strategy, 2015

Macleod S, Sharp C, Bernardinelli D et al, *Supporting the attainment of disadvantaged pupils: Articulating success and good practice, Research Report,* NFER, 2015

Matthews P et al, *Freedom to lead: A study of outstanding primary school leadership in England,* National College for Teaching and Leadership, 2014

Matthews P and Headon M, *Multiple gains: An independent evaluation of Challenge Partners' peer reviews of schools,* UCL Institute of Education, 2015

Morrish A, *The art of standing out: School transformation, to greatness and beyond,* John Catt, 2016

Myatt M, *High challenge low threat: How the best leaders find the balance,* John Catt, 2016

National Audit Office, *Funding for disadvantaged pupils: Report by the Comptroller and Auditor-General,* NAO, 2015

National College for School Leadership, *Executive heads: Summary report,* NCSL, 2010

National College for Teaching and Leadership, *Powerful professional learning: A school leader's guide to joint practice development,* NCTL, 2016

Ofsted, *Grant maintained schools 1989-92,* HMSO, 1993

Ofsted, *Twelve outstanding secondary schools: Excelling against the odds,* HMSO, 2009

Ofsted, *Twenty outstanding primary schools: Excelling against the odds,* HMSO, 2009

Ofsted, *Twelve outstanding special schools: Excelling through inclusion,* HMSO, 2009

Ofsted, *The London Challenge,* HMSO, 2010

Ofsted, *The pupil premium: How schools used the funding,* HMSO, 2012

Ofsted, *The pupil premium: How schools are spending the funding successfully to maximise achievement,* HMSO, 2013

Ofsted, *Unseen children: access and achievement twenty years on,* HMSO, 2013

Ofsted, *The pupil premium: An update,* HMSO, 2014

O'Neill O, *A question of trust, the Reith Lectures 2002,* Cambridge University Press, 2002

Peacock A, *Assessment for learning without limits*, Open University Press, 2016

Robinson V, *Student-centred leadership*, Wiley, 2011

Rowland M, *An updated practical guide to the pupil premium*, John Catt, second edition, 2015

Shechtman N et al, *Promoting grit, tenacity and perseverance: Critical factors for success in the 21st century*, US Department of Education Office of Educational Technology, 2013

Secondary Heads Association, *Towards intelligent accountability for schools*, SHA, 2003

Sharples J et al, *Making best use of teaching assistants*, Education Endowment Foundation, 2015

Social Market Foundation, *Educational inequalities in England and Wales*, SMF, 2016

Social Mobility Commission, *State of the nation 2014: social mobility and child poverty in Great Britain*, HMSO, 2014

Sutton Trust, *Improving the impact of teachers on pupil achievement in the UK*, Sutton Trust, 2011

Sutton Trust, *Missing talent*, Sutton Trust, 2015

Teaching Schools Council, *Effective pupil premium reviews*, Teaching Schools Council, second edition, 2016

Warwick Commission, *Enriching Britain: culture, creativity and growth*, University of Warwick, 2015

Webster R et al, *Maximising the impact of teaching assistants: guidance for school leaders and teachers*, Routledge, 2015

Wiliam D, *Leadership for teacher learning: Creating a culture where all teachers improve so that all students succeed*, Abe Books, 2016

Acknowledgements

This book draws on my experience of school leadership, as teacher, senior leadership team member and headteacher in the north-east of England, where I worked with many talented teachers and school leaders. My 12 years as general secretary of the Secondary Heads Association (which changed its name to the Association of School and College Leaders in 2005) brought me into contact not only with the school leaders I worked with and represented, but also with just about every politician and civil servant who made national education policy, as well as academics, leaders of other teacher unions and education organisations, and many international educationists. Since I retired from ASCL in 2010, I have met or worked with people in children's organisations, the Children's Commissioners of the UK countries and Ireland, and thousands of teachers and school leaders.

It is from so many of the people I have met on this leadership journey that I have learnt so much. They are far too numerous to list here. Some of them will know from reading this book who they are; but many others will not recall the conversation or event that added a piece to the jigsaw of experience represented in these pages. I have been privileged to have worked closely with some of the best and most inspiring members of the education service, from superb teachers at Framwellgate Moor, Bede School and Durham Johnston, to wonderful colleagues at ASCL and the National College for School Leadership, exceptional senior civil servants and committed politicians. I am indebted to them all.

I owe many thanks to several people who read through large parts of the first draft of this book and whose wise comments have been incorporated – Geoff Barton, Jill Berry, Andy Buck, David Crossley, Stef Edwards, Robert Hill, Steve Munby, Marc Rowland and my wife, Sue. I owe a particular debt of gratitude to Sue, whose wisdom and experience of education have over many years kept my feet on the ground when my thinking was in the clouds, given me some of my best quotes in the media and supported me at every stage of my leadership journey.

Glossary of abbreviations

APU   Assessment of Performance Unit

ASCL   Association of School and College Leaders (formerly SHA)

CBI   Confederation of British Industry

CfBT   Centre for British Teachers

CIEA   Chartered Institute of Educational Assessors

CPD   Continuing professional development

CSE   Certificate of Secondary Education

CTC   City Technology College

DfE   Department for Education

EBacc   English Baccalaureate

ECM   Every Child Matters

EEF   Education Endowment Foundation

EFA   Education Funding Agency

FSM   Free school meals

GCE   General Certificate of Education

GCSE   General Certificate of Secondary Education

GM   Grant-Maintained Schools

GTC   General Teaching Council

HMI	Her Majesty's Inspectorate and Her Majesty's Inspector
ITT	Initial teacher training
JPD	Joint practice development
LA	Local Authority
LEA	Local Education Authority
LLE	Local Leader of Education
LMS	Local Management of Schools
MAT	Multi-Academy Trust
NAHT	National Association of Head Teachers
NASUWT	National Union of Schoolmasters / Union of Women Teachers
NCSL	National College for School Leadership
NCTL	National College for Teaching and Leadership
NEET	Not in education, employment or training
NGA	National Governors' Association
NLE	National Leader of Education
NLG	National Leader of Governance
OECD	Organisation for Economic Co-operation and Development
QA	Quality assurance
QCA	Qualifications and Curriculum Authority
QCDA	Qualifications and Curriculum Development Agency
RSA	Royal Society of Arts
RSC	Regional Schools Commissioner
SCS	Schools Co-operative Society
SEND	Special education needs and disability
SHA	Secondary Heads Association
SIP	School Improvement Partner
SLE	Specialist Leader of Education

SSAT	Specialist Schools and Academies Trust
TDA	Training and Development Agency for Schools
TES	Times Educational Supplement
TLA	Teaching, learning and assessment